THE LORD IS...
A Prayer And Devotional Guide

Book 1 of Lessons From The Father Series

S.D. Simms

M☩ Zion Ridge Press
Books Off the Beaten Path

www.MtZionRidgePress.com

Mt Zion Ridge Press LLC
295 Gum Springs Rd, NW
Georgetown, TN 37366
https://www.mtzionridgepress.com

ISBN 13: 978-1-962862-63-9
Published in the United States of America
Publication Date: March 1, 2025
Copyright: © 2023 S.D. Simms

Editor-In-Chief: Michelle Levigne
Executive Editor: Tamera Lynn Kraft
Cover art design by Tamera Lynn Kraft
Cover Art Copyright by Mt Zion Ridge Press LLC © 2025

TABLE OF CONTENTS

PREFACE

Sharon Simms is one of the most down-to-earth Christians I have ever met and coupled with her ability to discern and understand Scripture, she's a very gifted woman.

God has led Sharon on a journey through loss and pain, yet she hasn't wasted time murmuring and groaning. Instead, she has bowed at the feet of Jesus, praising Him and asking how she can best serve Him. One of the ways she's done this is by learning who He and His Father are.

Having listened to and watched numerous devotional videos by Sharon over the last few years, I was not at all surprised to learn God had called her to create with Him the writing of these daily devotionals.

For those of you who may be unfamiliar with what a devotional is, let's define it from its roots.

Devote: *to give or apply one's attention, time, or self to an activity, cause, or person. In this instance, the one true God.*

Devotion: *ardent acts of religious observances or prayer-- In this instance, time spent getting to know who God is.*

Devotional: *a short religious service individually or a collective observance or participation in readings and/or prayer. In this instance, time with God.*

Journal: *a personal record of experiences, occurrences, and reflections kept daily or regularly. In this instance, your reflections as you understand who God is.*

With her Master, Sharon Simms has created a forty-day devotional journal. Each day's short reading is encapsulated as a *journey* into the study of the names of God, including a page for each with questions for *your* reflections. She's allowed you to internalize and write your thoughts and reactions.

I challenge you, even the busiest of readers, to devote twenty or more minutes over each of the next forty days, asking the Lord to open your eyes and heart to the depths of Him in this study.

Apply yourself to learning who God truly is by taking this forty-day journey with Sharon and Him.

Joy Avery Melville
Award-Winning Author, Mentor, & Freelance Editor

ACKNOWLEDGMENTS

I can do all things through Christ who strengthens me day by day. Humble gratitude to the One who owns my very breath. May this offering please and glorify Him. He placed family, friends, co-workers, church family, and strangers in strategic intersections of my life seasons. Two are better than one for a good return of labor, and a threefold cord isn't fast broken. I sincerely thank everyone for your part on a team that routed a dream into reality.

Thank you to my parents, from whom I gleaned a love for reading, Ms. Bruno, a third-grade teacher who fanned the flames for storytelling, and my first playmates and audience, siblings and first cousins, for allowing me to entertain them with my imagination.

Hearty thanks go to Neil Dumas, who suggested that Joy Massenburge and I meet. Her overflowing cup of the writing craft and love for people guided me through mistaken genre identity and inspired further passion for my calling. Joy and her daughter, Lotteice Greene, united their skills and talents to offer superb Mindset Coaching and Mentoring.

Being a part of an elite writers' group such as American Christian Fiction Writers (ACFW) on a national and local level proved invaluable. Cathy Rueter, the late Stacy Simmons, PJ Gover, and Lyndie Blevins supported, encouraged, and shared knowledge.

Joy Melville unveiled a plethora of tech skills and self-editing tips.

DiAnn Mills answered my questions. Thank you for suggesting the Blue Ridge Mountain Christian Writers Conference (BRMCWC). It opened a one-stop buffet of devotional education. Special thanks to Beth Patch, Katy Kauffman, Josie Siler, and every author I interacted with. We're blessed with momentous times in our lifespans, and the afternoon I met Lori Marrett and Cindy Sproles will forever be stamped as a divine appointment. They skim away dross, smooth rough edges, and picture a finished design.

Wendy Smelley, best friend, supporter, encourager, and prayer warrior, you are a jewel.

Without the team behind me, I wouldn't have traveled this far.

REFLECTIONS

Slow Leaks

Contractors installed new gas lines in Jacklyn's neighborhood. One of the workers shut off the supply to her house until they'd completed updating the piping on that section. Once reconnected, an inspection showed a slow leak. A company rep told Jacklyn that her gas would remain shut off. It took several days to pinpoint the exact location of the seepage. Our spiritual strength can sustain a gradual leak, too. However, we don't stop power from the main source as the men did with the gas. Instead, we run to the Lord for a refuel. Sights, sounds, and actions in this world via social media, conversations, and the news create and perpetuate wear and tear. The Word of God renews our strength and hope, which plug spiritual leaks.

But those who hope in the Lord will renew their strength.
Isaiah 40:31a

Discerning God's Voice

God told Adam, "You are free to eat from any tree in the garden, but you must not eat from the tree of the knowledge of good and evil." The serpent used his intellect to deceive Eve and Adam into questioning God's authority: "Did God say you can't eat from any tree?" The couple knew full well what their Creator had commanded. A troublemaker's tone, question, and one keyword produced doubt and subsequent disobedience. May we learn from the example of our first ancestors to ignore the noise of doubt, discouragement, and discontent the enemy plants to thwart purpose and vision. Listen. Discern and obey the Lord's voice. His will always agree with the Word and lead us to follow Jesus. (Ref. Gen. 2:1, 5; 3:1-2)

God Heard the Women

God ordered Moses to take a census of the men of Israel who were at least age twenty and able-bodied for warfare. They were numbered by tribes and then listed by sons within each tribe. Within Joseph's tribe, Zelophehad, who died during the wilderness journey, left five daughters but no sons. God commanded Moses to divide the Promised Land by the census count. The larger population inherited more than the smaller, but the five women were excluded altogether. Things changed when the ladies showed up at the tent for a meeting with the prophet, priest, and entire congregation. They pleaded their case based on their father's good character. Then followed up with a reasonable question: "Why should his name be removed from the family tree because he hadn't sired sons?" Zelophehad's daughters honored their raising by respectfully approaching and standing before God's tabernacle, Moses, the priest, and their elders.

When they asked for their father's portion of land, Moses checked with God. He heard the women and agreed. The Lord implemented a law on that day to protect future daughters: If a man who had no sons died, his inheritance would pass to the daughter. Mahlah, Noah, Hoglah, Milcah, and Tirzah approached the Lord's presence with humility. God listened and honored their request. Just as He heard these ladies, His ear bends to our whispers, cries, or inner moans.

Grant us boldness to come to You, Almighty, and a heart that seeks to do Your will. In Jesus' name, Amen.

(Ref. Num. 26:2, 33; 27:1-8)

Food for Thought

A carton of blueberries tumbled onto my kitchen floor, and a bag of sweet potatoes ripped when I pulled them from a grocery bag. On my knees gathering the vulnerable fruit, I wondered what lesson the Lord needed me to learn. Until I got up. My body squeaked, like *The Wonderful Wizard of Oz*'s Tin Man, as I eased down. The Lord picked me right up.

He can and will lift us out of physical and spiritual mishaps. Lean on Him today. He is our light and salvation, a rock in a weary land, and a refuge in times of trouble.

The Lord upholds all who fall and lifts all who are bowed down.
Psalm 145:14

Prayer:
Wondrous Father and Creator, petitions for blessings are lifted for the one who reads and studies this work. Anoint them with power and grace to comprehend the depth of Your infinite love. May it refresh, build up, and renew

the faint and weary, strengthen the weak, and restore those worn down with burdens. Lord, transform scars of the past into their path to their new identity in You, not the yesterdays. May each reader grasp that in You, we are enough. Heal those bound in addictions and habits. Grant their families wisdom and perseverance. May Your loving kindness capture the hearts of these devotional readers. Listen, oh Lord, show up and show out. Bless them to hear Your voice and be encouraged, despite trials, the enemy, and our flesh. You have a promised land for Your children. May Your one-time works inspire them to believe You're everything we need every moment of our lives. Thank You for creating us for good works. Your will be done on earth just as it is in Heaven. In Jesus' name, Amen.

Day One

EL SHAMA — THE LORD IS — GOD WHO HEARS

This poor man called, and the LORD heard him; he saved him out of all his troubles. **Psalm 34:6 (NIV)**

I lay on a gurney in an antiseptic ER room, waiting for a doctor. Across the hall, a young woman cradled a crying infant on her shoulder. Though she rocked and patted, the baby's wailing increased. Its tiny arms with tightened fists flailed the air. How marvelous that one so small innately knew to project his discomfort. Meanwhile, I, an adult, fretted in sole self-pity. No one showed up to hug me and listen to my expressions of pain. Someone would have if I'd sounded an alert. The Lord used a babe to illustrate that we're never alone. He hears our cries. Terror gripped David and constrained him to cry for help.

Jealousy drove King Saul to hunt for him as a hungry lion sought its prey. David panicked and fled from Nob to Gath to escape the king's murderous scheme. News of his presence spread like wildfire. The one who'd killed thousands more than Saul showed up at Gath. Renown made it impossible to hide out there, so David concocted a plan to appear insane before Achish, the ruler of that town. Disgusted by the drooling man's appearance, Achish dismissed him.

Imagine the emotions swirling inside a young man on the run from one he loved and feared. Place yourself in his proverbial shoes of loneliness, hunger, and physical exhaustion. David stumbled to the ground and cried out to the Lord for relief. He referred to himself as "this poor man" to suggest humility. Poor in this context acknowledged total dependence upon God. Psalm 34 records a tribute of thanksgiving from David. He knew God heard his call.

Like God, the medical staff heard the baby's cries and entered the baby's room. The door closed. Gradually, the little one ceased crying.

Amidst a health emergency, my feelings of self-pity overpowered sound reasoning. I should have called on the ever-present God instead of sulking in misery. When I sought His comfort, He answered and sent family and healing. God understands our weaknesses. Speak in faith with the El Shama. He will hear your pleas.

Prayer: *LORD, You hear every wail. May we love and trust You. Amen.*

Journal Page — Day One

El Shama — The Lord is the God Who Hears

This poor man called, and the LORD heard him; he saved him out of all his troubles. Psalm 34:6 (NIV)

1. God used the incessant cry of a baby to drag me out of the mire of self-pity.
How has He redirected your thoughts in times of trouble?

2. Write an acrostic for the word heard:

H=
E=
A=
R=
D=

3. Why did David describe himself as "this poor man"?

4. I know He hears me because:

Additional Scriptures

This is the confidence we have in approaching God: that if we ask anything according to His will, He hears us. 1 John 5:14 (NIV)

Day Two

JEHOVAH JIREH — THE LORD IS OUR PROVIDER

But whose delight is in the law of the LORD, and who meditates on his law, day, and night. Psalm 1:2 (NIV)

A brisk chill and relics of the last song I played before I drifted off the night before greeted me this morning. I stretched and slid to my knees by the bedside. "Thank You, Father, for a new beginning, great mercy, and every blessing. What would You have me do today?"

I pushed up from my knees, piled pillows against the headboard, and leaned against them. I reached for the Bible lying beside me. An attempt to reconcile with my daughter had failed. Again. Without fellowship, communication would not be restored. *Show me how to reach her.* The request lingered in thought while I read Bible pages, searching for answers. The word "delight" in Psalm 1 caught my attention. I paused and sat forward, adjusting pillows behind my back. Tingles coursed a highway along my arms. Anticipation kindled a flame of hopefulness. Delight means to receive great pleasure and joy from something or someone.

I do experience profound joy in studying and meditating on God's word. Day and night, it supplies peace and reminds me that I'm never alone. Even when I'm sad about losing loved ones and relationships, I know that the Lord is my provider because He has filled my void and longing for time spent with a daughter. He placed a young lady into my life, and we have developed a close bond.

A prominent woman from Shunem offered Elisha, a man of God, rest and food each time he traveled past. One day, word came of a seven-year famine. Elisha warned the woman and her household to journey somewhere safe. They obeyed and hurried to the land of the Philistines. After the famine ended, the woman and her son traveled home. She appealed to the king to reclaim her property.

In a God-nugget moment, Gehazi, a servant of Elisha, also appeared before the king. He advised the ruler of all the great works Elisha the prophet had done. Imagine Gehazi visiting the king and glimpsing in person a young man whom God brought back to life, using Elisha. The servant might aid the man's mother in regaining her land if he told how she'd ministered to the man of God all those years. "This woman supplied food and lodging for God's prophet. The young man is her only son. One she yearned for. God sent word through Elisha that she would bear a child. The woman's son grew up and fell dead, but Elisha brought him back to life."

The king listened to the remarkable story recounted by the woman and Gehazi. He returned all the Shunamite's possessions plus income accrued from the field from the day she left up to that very moment.

God provides physical and mental revival as I study His Word and participate in Celebrate Recovery. This peer-supported Christian program aids participants in healthy recuperation from hurts, habits, and hang-ups through principles of the Bible. When I stopped by to check on them, an elderly couple from church furnished helpful information about a surgeon.

The Lord blessed me with a present and active daughter in my life. She calls and visits and makes me smile. He continues to illustrate gracious provision for me as a widow, just as He did for the Shunamite woman. In my younger years, I'd listened to faithful elders at the church discuss how God "walked and talked with them." One, Mrs. Inez remarked, "Baby, I don't worry about a thing. The Lord takes care of me." She knew from experience, just as I'm sharing now. Nothing is too small or big for God. Bring all your concerns and requests to the One who cares and will provide. Trust in His promises.

Prayer: *Father, You are our provider. Our hope and our eyes are on You. In Jesus' name, Amen.*

Journal Page — Day Two

Jehovah Jireh — The Lord Is — Our Provider

But whose delight is in the law of the Lord, and who meditates on his law, day and night. Psalm 1:2 (NIV)

1. How can you delight in the Lord when you open your eyes?

2. Acrostic for Meditate to remind you of the Lord's provision and His Word:

M=
E=
D=
I=
T=
A=
T=
E=

3. What provision do you need from the Lord?

4. How has God provided above and beyond what you have requested?

Additional Scripture & Reflection

Now to Him who is able to do immeasurably more than all we ask or imagine, according to His power that is at work within us. Ephesians 3:20 (NIV)

Day Three

JEHOVAH TOWB – THE LORD IS GOOD

Taste and see that the LORD *is good...* Psalm 34:8a. (NIV)

Eating healthier requires a lifestyle change. No more random strolling down grocery aisles and impulse buying. Instead, shopping becomes a challenge, involving searching out eligible items and reading labels. Searching for the good stuff to entice our appetite requires research and more time. Pit stops to the fast-food drive-by are replaced with at-home meal prep. Eat balanced meals and purposefully maximize the chewing to enjoy and then digest. A heightened sense of flavor and texture can be experienced anew.

Confessing Christ as our Lord changes lives, too. We yearn for more than easy substitutes. Our appetites crave spiritual food to dive into with both hands like guests at a crawfish boil. We want to plant our proverbial elbows on a table and pick it apart, word by word, verse by verse, just as we'd tear into a juicy crawfish. Go past the outer shell and dig in to taste all the meat of God's Word. I wonder if that's what David had in mind when he wrote about tasting the Lord's goodness.

"Taste and see that the Lord is good" is the first half of verse 8 in Psalm 34. The King invited us to use two of our senses and know the goodness of God. The best way to get to know someone is to spend time in fellowship to build a relationship gradually. How do we taste and see God's virtue? Good question. Imagine sinking your teeth into a fresh, ripe peach, a succulent morsel of meat, or a savory spoon of fragrant soup. Next, think of these food items as the word of God.

What if we didn't shove our physical nourishment down so fast? Instead, we should take time to chew on it and reflect on its texture, flavor, and pleasant effect. A deeper appreciation will transform a nonchalant attitude to thankfulness. Indeed, we have tasted the Word at just the right time and found it satisfying for our souls. Despite my inconsistencies, the Lord is good all the time. He slathers us with love and mercy as one slathers mayo or mustard on a favorite sandwich. Crack open a Bible today and taste His goodness.

Where do you need a taste of goodness today? Work, school, and extracurricular activities can keep us on the run. Choose one meal a day to sit and savor your physical and spiritual food. Sharing your insights with a co-worker, friend, or fellow student is a marvelous way to invite them to taste the goodness.

Prayer: *Thank You, Lord, for every perfect gift. May we remember to reflect on Your goodness and mercy as we partake of food and drink. In Jesus' name, Amen.*

Journal Page – Day Three

Jehovah Towb – The Lord Is Good

Taste and see that the LORD is good... Psalm 34:8a. (NIV)

1. What is God's goodness?

2. Where do you see the Lord's goodness?

3. Have you tasted it?

4. Define refuge as it relates to eating at the LORD's table.

Additional Scriptures

Give thanks to the LORD, for he is good; his love endures forever. Psalm 107:1 (NIV)

Day Four

THE LORD IS — OUR GUARD

Set a guard over my mouth, LORD; keep watch over the door of my lips.
Psalm 141:3 (NIV)

The dress slid over my hips like soft cream cheese on a bagel. It still fit after two years. Now to get it zipped from the lower back to the top. That was one of the liabilities of living alone. I once watched a female character on a comedy show slide up a bedroom wall to zip up an evening gown. Yes, I tried it — and no, it didn't work. While I twisted and turned, wrestling with that zipper, a sobering thought popped into my mind about my mouth. Of late, I'd had trouble zipping it before offensive words slipped out. Someone might invent a tool to alleviate the dress problem in the future, but only God can guard my mouth.

Have you spoken rash words in an emotional midnight and wanted to swallow them back after the dawn of your calm? You're not alone, dear one. All of us have said things we've later regretted, if truth be told. I can't do this, or things will never change. Does any of this dialogue ring familiar? Sighs of folly seep from our lips, unbridled by the usual wisdom when we're agitated. Words like this crush self-esteem, pummel faith, and condemn. They do not build one up.

In Judges 11, Jephthah, a valiant warrior and Gileadite, received an offer from the elders of Gilead. The people would make him commander of his homeland if he defeated the Ammonites. Jephthah agreed with the terms and attempted peaceful negotiations with the king of the Ammonites. The king refused to listen. On the way to battle, the Gileadite devised a plan to secure a win. He offered a vow uncalled for to the Lord. That promise cost Jephthah his only child, a daughter, her future, and him his heirs.

Choose life by employing our lips with words to build up and encourage one another. If unkind thoughts enter your mind, plead with the Lord to take them away and refrain from giving them a voice. Don't jabber like Jephthah. Just zip it.

Prayer: Lord, guard my mouth and keep my thoughts. May my inner self reflect the heart of You and overflow to others. Amen

Journal Page — Day Four

The Lord is — Our Guard

Set a guard over my mouth, LORD; keep watch over the door of my lips.
Psalm 141:3 (NIV)

1. Would you serve beloved family members or friends a meal of rotten or tainted food? Of course not! Why do we expose them to filth spat from our lips?

2. List words to encourage others.

3. Have you suffered hurt because of something someone said to or about you? How did you react?

4. How can we turn negative interactions into positive outcomes?

5. What image comes to mind when you read "keep watch"? How does the image promote an attitude of thinking before speaking?

Additional Scriptures

Those who guard their mouths and their tongue keep themselves from calamity. Proverbs 21:23 (NIV)

Day Five

THE LORD IS — OUR PROMISE KEEPER

The Lord is trustworthy in all He promises and faithful in all He does.
Psalm 145:13b. (NIV)

The slate-gray stones caught my attention. Positioned under a massive live oak, they symbolized the sacrifices of veterans across the county. One stone per division of the United States armed forces was engraved with its seal and the names of veterans from our county. Soldiers' names were listed under the war era in which they served. The stones commemorated brave men and women who answered the call to leave the comfort of home for dangerous expeditions. Architects positioned the memorial on the courthouse's front lawn to be noticed. Passersby pause and reflect on individuals, families, and armed service units' contributions to our nation's freedoms.

Jacob, son of Isaac, set out for Haran in search of a wife. He journeyed all day and stopped for the night when the sun set. Exhausted from the journey, Jacob searched for a stone for a pillow and slept soundly. He dreamed of a ladder that stretched from the ground to the sky. Angels of God climbed up and down it. God appeared and declared incredible promises. He assured Jacob that He was the same Lord of his grandfather and father.

The next morning, an awestruck Jacob set his stone pillow up as a pillar. He poured oil on it and renamed the area the House of God. The future groom might have recollected stories of his father, Isaac, who had testified of his and Abraham's lives and the Lord's provision and faithfulness even in strange lands. Now, he'd experienced a personal encounter with the Lord and commemorated it with a memorial stone and name. When we enter foreign territories for a new job, school, location, or a new season of life, it's good to know we're not alone.

Most of us like the stability of a place to call home. The Lord assured Jacob that He would bring him back to this place where he had laid his head as his home. The never-changing, impartial God still honors His promises.

I've claimed God's Word never to leave nor forsake us in times of loneliness, pain, and sorrow. I ran my fingers across some of the names I recognized from the Vietnam era and thought about the survivors and those who paid the ultimate price. One, Charlie, a childhood friend's brother, had promised to fix our bikes when he returned.

Make every effort to let your yes be yes and your no be no. If you covenant in a personal relationship or business deal, treat each transaction as unto the Lord. Know that the divine Promise Keeper sends or allows all that happens in the lives of His children.

Prayer: *Father, we are grateful that Your promises are true. In Jesus' name, Amen.*

Journal Page — Day Five

The Lord is — Our Promise Keeper

The Lord is trustworthy in all He promises and faithful in all He does. Psalm 145:13b (NIV)

1. List memorials you have seen.

2. Why did Jacob make a memorial out of the stone?

3. What does a promise from God mean to you?

4. What promise(s) have you made to God? Yourself? Others?

5. What characteristics can enable you to keep your promise?

Additional Scriptures

I will not violate my covenant or alter what my lips have uttered. Psalm 89:34 (NIV)

Day Six

PART 1: FROM STRENGTH TO POTTER
THE LORD IS—OUR STRENGTH

God is our refuge and strength, an ever-present help in trouble. **Psalm 46:1** (NIV)

The garage door creaked while it gradually rose. As I pulled into the garage, my vehicle headlights reflected off a jumbled pile. Boxes of laminate flooring had spilled into my parking space. A sigh of dread matched a knot of discontent in my stomach as I peered through the windshield. The boxes languished like toppled Jenga blocks or giant dominoes. *Lord, help.*

Way past exhausted and the night far spent, neither game inspired enthusiasm. Instead, a heaviness settled in my chest. Earlier in the day, a well-meaning relative stacked the boxes haphazardly in a rush. I bit back voicing concern out of appreciation. Now, I moaned in regret. Why hadn't I spoken up? I groaned at the low back pain. God's grace strengthened me to lift each cumbersome box.

How ironic that my groaning mimicked the creaking door. Although decades old and worn out, the door continued to serve its purpose. I, too, have advanced in years, though spiritually, I am youthful. What a blessing it is to call upon Abba Father for every need. The more we realize our weaknesses and depend on Him, the greater our awareness of His omnipotent strength.

God promised the children of Israel a land flowing with milk and honey. He assigned the prophet Moses to lead them and ordered Moses to send a man from each of the twelve tribes to spy out the land and bring back a report. The spies discovered that all God promised about the land proved true, but the presence of giants and others who occupied the area frightened them. Ten spies forgot in whose power and strength they'd succeeded thus far. Their report to Moses predicted doom. Joshua and forty-year-old Caleb begged to differ. Caleb announced, "Don't rebel against the Lord. He is with us."

Moses replied, "May the Lord's strength be displayed as you have declared." (Num.14:17) God promised Caleb an inheritance from the land he searched for. He and Joshua were the only original sojourners to reach the land of abundance forty-five years later.

Joshua guided the children of his former peers into the land flowing with milk and honey. God had chosen the son of Nun to succeed Moses. At eighty-five years old, Caleb remained vigorous and as strong as four decades before. He anticipated no problem taking over the land he'd inherited. Even though giants possessed large, fortified cities in Hebron, Caleb continued to rely on the Lord's strength. "I will drive them out just as He said." (Josh. 14:12) Nothing seems too hard or impossible when we rely on God's power.

We can rely on God as our strength. His presence, provident care, and power will fortify us physically and emotionally. Trials can be endured, and enemies of temptation and opposition resisted in boldness, knowing we're not alone. Time in the wilderness can also bring deliverance and refreshing and draw us closer to our Creator. The Lord even proved to be my Strength when moving those heavy boxes.

Prayer: *Father, demonstrate Your power in the wilderness of our lives. May we draw from Your well of strength and hope. In Jesus' name, Amen.*

Journal Page—Day Six

Part 1: From Strength to Potter
The Lord Is—Our Strength

God is our refuge and strength, an ever-present help in trouble. Psalm 46:1 (NIV)

1. What does the word "ever-present" mean to you?

2. What comes to mind when you hear "strength"?

3. Describe your ideal physical place of safety on Earth.

4. How may God's strength be displayed in you?

5. Repeat the scripture above and place your name before the word "trouble":

6. God is our refuge and strength, an ever-present help in _____'s trouble.

Additional Scriptures

So do not fear, for I am with you. Do not be dismayed, for I am your God.
I will strengthen you and help you. I will uphold you with my righteous right hand. Isaiah 41:10 (NIV)

Day Seven

PART 2: FROM STRENGTH TO POTTER
THE LORD IS – THE POTTER

But the pot he was shaping from the clay was marred in his hands, so, the potter formed it into another pot, shaping it as seemed best to him. Jeremiah 18:4 (NIV)

What possessed me to clean up a gigantic wood spill right after back injections? The discharge instructions prescribed rest, copious fluid intake, and charting pain intensity for the evening. Who could rest when it sounded like half your house just blew up? A loud *wham* and clattering commotion sent my heart racing and me rocking to investigate. What a mess. Boxes of flooring and miscellaneous woodcuts, some with nails, tumbled and splattered across the hallway. I would have left it if it hadn't blocked the pathway to my bedroom. The moment I stooped and attempted to lift a box of laminate flooring, sharp pain radiated from my lower back, and numbness claimed my left foot. Big mistake.

Nail-studded trim bounced off another box and slid past the bathroom. A sharp pain shot across my back, and I froze, leaning against a wall. When it relented, I shoved and dragged what I could back to one side. It's challenging to take care of yourself and your home, too. Wouldn't it be nice to be made over again? Did you ever desire a redo? God sent one of His messengers to a potter's house to demonstrate that He can do anything.

The Lord had a word for the house of Israel. To illustrate the message, he sent the Prophet Jeremiah to a potter's house. There's nothing like personal heart knowledge of what you're appointed to share with others. As the potter wrought a vessel on the wheel that might have finished too stiff, misshapen, or rocky, he would place it back on the wheel and redo it. Jeremiah heard the Lord's message. Just as the human potter can mold clay, the Father can fashion nations and kingdoms as He pleases.

Even more, clay appears as a lump form. We have form and matter. God created us with freedom of choice. As the potter may use one vessel for one thing and another for a different function, the sovereign Lord can place us on His wheel of grace and mercy, fashion us with love, and rightly judge us accordingly. He has molded me into a vessel of encouragement for those suffering from illness and pain. God answered my prayer—not in the manner I'd asked, yet more fruitful. He increased my faith and perseverance through the darkness of pain. The new me is a better listener, gives more grace and patience, and my lenses view others through the love of Jesus.

Despite your discomfort, repeat a verse such as, "I can do all things through Christ who strengthens me." Ask the Lord to mold you into the vessel He designed you to be. Yield to the Potter's will.

Prayer: *Father, make and mold me into a vessel pleasing to You. I pray to care for Your temple daily. In Jesus' name. Amen.*

Journal Page—Day Seven

Part 2: From Strength to Potter
The Lord is—The Potter

But the pot he was shaping from the clay was marred in his hands, so, the potter formed it into another pot, shaping it as seemed best to him. **Jeremiah 18:4 (NIV)**

1. What kind of pot are you?

2. Define the term "marred" in your words.

3. Write down the first thing you visualized when you heard "marred."

4. Do you yearn for remolding? If so, in what area(s)?

5. What negative experiences come to mind that have shaped your life?

6. Is there someone else you're praying for God to remold?

Additional Scriptures

Yet you, Lord, are our Father. We are the clay. You are the potter.
We are all the work of your hand. **Isaiah 64:8 (NIV)**

Day Eight

JEHOVAH ELOHIM — THE LORD IS THE GOD OF CREATION

The heavens declare the glory of God; the skies proclaim the work of his hands. Psalm 19:1 (NIV)

Yesterday, our pastor reminded us how nature declared the Glory of God with a quote from Psalm 19:1. The next day, on my way home from choir practice, the heavens sang, "Good evening." The melody chorused in a group of creamy white clouds gathered low over the western horizon. Their launderer's hue, backdropped by brilliant sunrays, graced the lighter-than-light blue sky and my heart. I smiled the rest of the way, accompanied by an overhead symphony declaring God's glory.

We don't all speak a common language, yet the stars, moon, and sun convey universal enlightenment. David declared, "There is no speech nor language where their voice is not heard." Psalm 19:3

When I read this, it called to mind Jesus' rebuke to the Pharisees in Luke 19:40: "If they keep quiet, the stones will cry out." Vocal opponents of Christ had reprimanded a crowd for praising Jesus. Humanity is powerless to silence nature's salute to the Creator.

Imagine the proclamation of God's glory by the wild blue yonder, illustrious sunrises, and golden sunsets. Ruminate on the exultation of a night sky resplendent with stars, a bright, full moon, and the din of summer katydids. Creation honors the Creator and Lord of all Who spoke a world into existence. Marvelous are the works that satisfy and thrill the gifts of sensory perception. If volcanoes and incredible waterfalls echo His majesty, how much more should humanity whom the Creator blessed with souls? Yes. Come, let us adore Him. It's our reasonable response as recipients of the gifts of nature and as those generated to exalt God in all we do.

Take a moment to reflect on the gifts of creation. The Lord loves us so much that He produced indescribable delights and formed us with senses to experience them.

Grab your Bible and choose a spot outside to read and meditate on passages like Psalm 19 and Genesis 1-3. The next time you're near a mirror, peer up close at the amazing and miraculous image reflected there. Consider its intricate and unique design and the Father who built it. May this compel an outburst of sincere thanks to the Lord, our Creator.

Prayer: *May the words of my mouth, the actions I take, and the thoughts of my heart be pleasing to You, Lord. Amen.*

Journal Page—Day Eight

Jehovah Elohim—The Lord is the God of Creation

The heavens declare the glory of God; the skies proclaim the work of his hands. Psalm 19:1 (NIV)

1. List four categories of creation.

2. When have you appreciated another person as God's creation?

3. What place draws you to appreciate nature's beauty and power as described in Psalm 19?

4. What does creation say to you about who God is?

Additional Scriptures

For since the creation of the world, God's invisible qualities—his eternal power and divine nature—have been seen, being understood from what has been made, so that people are without excuse. Romans 1:20 (NIV)

Psalm 19:1-3, Isaiah 43:7, Luke 19:40 (NIV)

Day Nine

THE LORD IS – OUR GOD OF COMFORT

Praise be to the God and Father of our Lord Jesus Christ, the Father of compassion and the God of all comfort... 2 Corinthians 1:3 (NIV)

My paternal grandparents graduated to heaven before I'd journeyed into adulthood and knew to voice appreciation for their hospitality and wisdom. In the narrow-bridged roads of Sunrise, a neighborhood in San Augustine, Texas, visitors to their working farm often received jovial greetings of, "Get out and come on in. Make yourselves at home." Grandpa offered his shady napping spot and shifted to a wooden porch swing, saying, "Here, get comfortable." Grandma sweetened the time with homemade teacakes and ice-cold, hand-churned buttermilk to wash down the cookies. Yum. Savor the burst of flavors on a delicious sun-sprinkled day with laughter and fellowship designed to make you feel at home.

The Apostle Paul invited Christians in Corinth and throughout Achaia to praise and adore the Lord as the Father of all comfort. In this context, "all comfort" is derived from a Greek term, *paraklesis*. It means to strengthen or help. *Fortis*, the Latin name, translates as brave. No doubt Paul wrote as a witness who'd experienced God's abundant solace firsthand. The former persecutor of the church endured rejection and beatings to fulfill God's call. Paul couldn't have stayed the course had the Lord not strengthened and encouraged the apostle for the journey before him. His consolation enabled him to bolster and reassure others from prison.

Sometimes, people would stop by Grandma and Grandpa's house on the way from town or after a funeral. Neighbors walked down the road. Trials and afflictions pebbled their life's journey. Were these random travelers searching for kind inspiration? Physical and spiritual sustenance? Or a comforting speech from those who could relate to their predicaments?

My grandparents imitated Paul in offering what the Lord gave them to sustain others: a shady spot to sit and rest on the front porch, food and drink refreshments, laughter, uplifting conversation, and their time. The Lord of all comfort has created us each with unique gifts to build up one another and glorify His name. Read 2 Corinthians 1 and ask God how to apply it to your life. Praise the Father for how He has consoled you. Prayerfully seek opportunities to offer consolation to others.

Prayer: *Father, thank You for all comforts. May I be a conduit for your consolation to those in need? In Jesus' name, Amen.*

Journal Page — Day Nine

The Lord is — Our God of Comfort

Praise be to the God and Father of our Lord Jesus ·Christ the Father of compassion and the God of all comfort... 2 Corinthians 1:3 (NIV)

1. List ways to praise the Father of all comfort.

2. What is significant about Paul's entire name for the Lord in verse 3 above?

3. How has the Lord comforted you?

4. Explain the difference between comfort in this text and the comfort of a well-worn shoe or bathrobe.

5. List ways you may comfort others.

Additional Scriptures

Even though I walk through the darkest valley, I will fear no evil, for you are with me; your rod and your staff, they comfort me. Psalm 23:4 (NIV)

Day Ten

THE LORD IS – OUR BOUNTIFUL GOD

And God is able to bless you abundantly, so that in all things at all times, having all that you need, you will abound in every good work. 2 Corinthians 9:8 (NIV)

The words, "And God is able..." washed tides of rejuvenation over my aching muscles. Tension eased off the back of my neck and shoulders. I repeated the words slowly and added phrases, "And God is able to give me peace that surpasses all understanding. And God is able to..." Excitement fluttered inside like butterflies. Oh, the possibilities. A friend read the title and asked, "Why are you writing about God being able? The title says, 'Our bountiful God.'" I smiled and answered, "Because another word for 'able' is 'superior,' and I believe superior God bountifully supplies every need."

The Corinthian church had eagerly pledged, from sincere hearts, to send financial aid to saints in need. A year later, Paul wrote to inform them that trustworthy brothers were headed to pick up their pledges. He'd included a disclaimer in the letter, so the church would understand that he remembered their willingness. Paul aimed to protect their integrity and not catch them unprepared.

Picture your family pledging a large donation one year in advance. No reminder phone call, text message, or calendar app to help you recall the date. One weekend when the banks are closed, you're surprised when someone shows up to collect. The apostle rekindled a desire to donate generously with a kind memo. He assured the flock that their bountiful God would replenish what they sowed and supply their needs beyond expectation. We can't out-give the Lord.

The four words that start the first paragraph still draw incredible bliss. They remind me that generous peace and wisdom are available. The Lord can and will give all we require. Corinthian believers volunteered financial support because they, too, understood this truth. When we comprehend our roles as stewards, not owners, the Lord utilizes us as channels of bounty. You may be asked to sacrifice time or material resources. Each sincere contribution triggers joy and thanksgiving from the givers. Recipients often pour out praise and glorify the Lord. Pray for guidance on how to steward resources and talent. Give generously. If you're in need, count on the bountiful God to supply.

Prayer: *Yes, Lord. You can do anything but fail. My soul magnifies Your holy name. May I share with others as You have richly blessed me with service and resources? In Jesus' name, Amen.*

Journal Page—Day Ten

The Lord is—Our Bountiful God

And God is able to bless you abundantly, so that in all things at all times, having all that you need, you will abound in every good work. 2 Corinthians 9:8 (NIV)

1. Define the word "bountiful" in your words.

2. How does God's bountifulness mean He can bless you abundantly?

3. List ways God can use you as a resource to bless others.

4. What motivates you to do good work?

Additional Scriptures

For it is God who works in you to will and to act in order to fulfill his good purpose. Philippians 2:13 (NIV)

Day Eleven

THE LORD IS — OUR GOD OF WISDOM

If any of you lacks wisdom, you should ask God, who gives generously to all without finding fault, and it will be given to you. James 1:5 (NIV)

Concern after concern swirled in my mind like leaves rustling about in blustery March winds. I rubbed at the tightness above my nose and between my eyes. Household repairs, time-consuming requests, and frustration at choices decided on by some family members consumed my mind. Looming deadlines added to the burdens. I needed knowledge on how best to eradicate the leaves of concern. "Lord, help." God invites us to seek His wisdom when we fall short. How blessed believers are to call on God and invoke His divine deliverance.

Wisdom is defined as a deep love and respect for God and an ability to relate spiritual truth to life's circumstances. Adam, our first ancestor, lacked the spiritual wisdom required to live daily as God purposed. "Lack," as used in the verse above, refers to a shortage in one's account, a deficit, if you will.

Let's consider other examples of the absence of comprehension and the dire danger of deficiency in godly wisdom. Consider a checking account with a low balance and an upcoming high draft amount for an electric bill. No money, no paid bill, and no electricity. How about body aches from a vitamin deficiency? It can result in sleep loss and poor performance at school or on the job. Vitamins must be purchased. However, God doles out wisdom free of charge to all who ask. He guarantees no reprimand.

I comprehend the Word on a deeper level when I spend quiet moments at the feet of God first. Contemplate establishing a daily time to talk and listen to the Lord. Ask Him for understanding in any matters that concern you. Nothing is too big or small. Share your heart. Thank Him for all He has done. Read the Word aloud a section at a time to comprehend, not just to check off a list. Ask God to hide it in your heart and reveal wondrous things. Just as the Father blew away my leaves of concern with gentle winds of wisdom, He promises His word as a haven of wisdom for you.

Prayer: *Father, grant me wisdom and courage to do those things that I should, the knowledge and stamina to withhold from those I shouldn't, and serenity of mind to understand You are still in control. In Jesus' name, Amen.*

Journal Page — Day Eleven

The Lord is — Our God of Wisdom

If any of you lacks wisdom, you should ask God, who gives generously to all without finding fault, and it will be given to you. James 1:5 (NIV)

1. Why does the author begin verse 5 with 'If'?

2. In your words, explain the difference between the wisdom of the world and God's wisdom.

3. How much comfort does the phrase "without finding fault" give you?

Prayer: *Father, I humbly lift the persons You ordained years ago to read this journal. Infuse their hearts and minds with the richness of knowledge to live and thrive as You purposed. Touch their bodies and spirits and emblazon a fire of boldness to share all they know about You with others. Strengthen them against the enemy's wiles, the world's trappings, and the weakness within. In Jesus' name, Amen*

Additional Scriptures

For the Lord gives wisdom. From his mouth come knowledge and understanding. Proverbs 2:6 (NIV)

Day Twelve

THE LORD IS — COMMANDER OF THE ARMY

All those gathered here will know that it is not by sword or spear that the Lord saves; for the battle is the Lord's, and he will give all of you into our hands. 1 Samuel 17:47 (NIV)

The church choir harmonized a melodious hymn of praise about soldiers in the army of the Lord. Words of the upbeat tune paid honor and glory to the commander. The lyrics generated a warm beat of thankfulness in my heart as I recalled how the Lord helped me defeat my giants of low self-worth and co-dependency with His inspired word. Verses from Psalms cut away the cloak of conquest. *Though an army besiege me, my heart will not fear. Though war break out against me, even then I will be confident.* Psalm 27:3 (NIV): *I praise you because I am fearfully and wonderfully made. Your works are wonderful. I know that full well. No weapon formed against me prospered with God as my strength.* Psalm 139:14 (NIV)

He crushed my giants just as He downed the Philistine giant at the hands of David.

Philistines represented five areas the Israelites did not wholeheartedly eradicate when they claimed their promised land. Like weeds and sin, the Philistines were difficult to get rid of. In 1 Samuel 17, the two armies camped on opposite mountains with a valley in between. Under Saul's command, the Israelites, including David's three older brothers, lined up to fight against their nemesis. David arrived in time to see a nine-foot giant Philistine challenge the Israelites to a one-on-one duel. Whoever won, that nation would be free.

The mammoth size of such a man sent Saul's army back to camp. Young David took on the challenge. He agreed to fight the giant in the strength of the Lord, along with a slingshot and five smooth stones. Guess what? It took only one stone. David informed the big guy, "This day, the Lord will deliver you into my hand, and I will cut your head off." He fired a stone from his sling, which landed dead center on the Philistine's forehead. David pulled the giant's sword from its sheath and sliced off his head. Everything David did, he accomplished in the Lord's power.

No matter what giants you face today, God can help you slay them. He reminded me that the Word is living and like a two-edged sword. My focus shifted from problems to faith in the One who can do everything except fail. Transfer your focal point. Instead of concentrating on how large or complicated a situation is, center your thoughts on the mighty Commander of the Army.

Prayer: *Father, King, Creator, and Giant Slayer, we can't thank You enough. We bow in Your mighty presence. Amen.*

Journal Page—Day Twelve

The Lord is—Commander of the Army

All those gathered here will know that it is not by sword or spear that the Lord saves; for the battle is the Lord's, and he will give all of you into our hands. 1 Samuel 17:47 NIV

1. What giants are you, or someone you love, facing?

2. How have you observed God making a way in the past?

3. What does a sword or spear represent in this verse?

4. The Philistines worshipped idol gods. They opposed the spiritual truths of our one true God. They were a constant source of agitation for the Israelites. What might the Philistines symbolize in your life?

5. Do you sense the Lord directing you to remove something?

Additional Scriptures

For I know the plans I have for you, declares the LORD, plans to prosper you and not to harm you, plans to give you hope and a future. Jeremiah 29:11 (NIV)

Day Thirteen

THE LORD IS—GOD WHO RENEWS OUR MINDS

Do not conform to the pattern of this world, but be transformed by the renewing of your mind. Then, you will be able to test and approve what God's will is—his good, pleasing, and perfect will. Romans 12:2 (NIV)

The outside of a local retail store gleamed with silver bells, bright red bows, and sparkling lights. The moment I stepped inside, the Christmas aura disappeared. Where were the decorations inside? I inched down one crowded display aisle after another. "The outside of the store looks great," I commented to a clerk behind a cluttered counter where I placed my items.

"Yeah." She pushed boxes aside. "I think we'll start inside tomorrow. I figured I'd clear out some junk and dust first."

I smiled. "You have to start somewhere."

Hezekiah desired to please the Lord with his leadership capacity. In the first year of his reign, King Hezekiah charged priests and Levites with sanctifying the work of removing pagan filth from the temple. The men gathered their brothers and consecrated their bodies and minds as the king commanded. The house of the Lord was cleaned, and the vessels returned to the altar.

Ahaz, his father, had reigned as king of Judah for sixteen years and revolted against God. He permitted the burning of children as human sacrifices, approved cast images of pagan idols, and took treasured vessels out of the temple to bribe the king of Assyria. He did not seek help from nor revere the Lord. This unlearned ruler closed the temple doors and sacrificed to strange gods, which provoked God's wrath. When King Ahaz died, he was buried in the city cemetery, not royal tombs. His son Hezekiah inherited the throne next.

With God's leadership, it only took sixteen days for Hezekiah to undo sixteen years of gross paganism created by Ahaz. He gathered the city rulers and rededicated the temple with sacrificial burnt offerings. Judah recalled the Lord's goodness, mercy, and great deeds as each solemn offering progressed. Genuine repentance and heart rehabilitation birthed humble hope. All the congregation celebrated with joy the restoration of the temple and a fresh start with the Lord. Respect and love for our Creator unlocked the door to a renewed mindset.

Hezekiah's spiritual rule illustrates the importance of regular dusting and clearing our minds. We can then receive the jewel of the Word, which works on our inner man. Our outer bodies light up like those silver bells when our hearts and minds are renewed.

Anything or anyone we think about more than God is an idol. When your thoughts are short-circuited by the flesh, the world, or Satan's schemes, draw near to the Lord. Completely surrender as a living sacrifice. Relax and release your walk, talk, and mind to the Father of renewal.

Prayer: *Father, help us remember that living to please You is the least we can do. In Jesus' name, Amen.*

Journal Page — Day Thirteen

The Lord is — God Who Renews Our Minds

Do not be conformed to this age, but be transformed by the renewing of Your mind, so that you may discern what is the good, pleasing, and perfect will of God. Romans 12:2 (NIV)

1. Where do you sense the Lord leading you toward renewal?

2. What does it mean to conform?

3. Use the word "discern" in a sentence. Define it in your own words.

4. What's another word for "complete" in this verse?

5. How can our minds be renewed?

6. Praises and prayer concerns:

Additional Scriptures

For everything in the world — the lust of the flesh, the lust of the eyes, and the pride of life — comes not from the Father but from the world. 1 John 2:16 (NIV)

Day Fourteen

EL SHADDAI—THE LORD IS THE ALL-SUFFICIENT GOD

How priceless is your unfailing love, O God! People take refuge in the shadow of your wings. Psalm 36:7 (NIV)

An ordinary Tuesday changed into anything but when I received the devastating news of two sweet friends' unexpected passing. Distracted by the grief, I sipped tea, unaware it contained a spice I'm allergic to, and suffered an excruciating reaction. Painful canker sores dotted my lips, gums, and inner cheeks. Hydrogen peroxide inflamed the situation.

One phone message from our church group thread that morning made me view Job on a deeper human level. God allowed Satan to play havoc with this righteous man. Satan claimed that Job's faithfulness to God depended on all the riches and family he enjoyed. The devil destroyed Job's children and livestock one day and afflicted his whole body with agonizing sores the next. Poor Job never understood why. There were moments when he cursed his birth and wanted to die because the grief and pain were unbearable, yet he maintained trust in God.

After the deaths and canker sores and knowing the inconsolable sorrow of burying a child, I related. The night our son left this world, the pain slammed me senseless. I remember wailing out, "I can't do this." Days and months afterward, my family and I struggled with shock, disbelief, and pain that sliced and jabbed our souls. God's sufficient grace picked us up and carried us through. We had no strength on our own. I know why Job refused to curse God or cave in as his wife suggested and the devil boasted. Despite people and things, Job knew God as his Father and provider. He trusted that the all-sufficient God could and would care for him as He promised. Job's story illustrates the believer's total dependence and faith in our all-sufficient, merciful God.

Satan supposed wrong that a true believer would deny God over something that doesn't belong to us in the first place. We're stewards, born into the world naked, and none depart for the grave with a U-Haul. El Shaddai transformed my mourning gray to vivid hues of purpose. God has allowed me to pray for and with those considering taking their lives, pray for other grieving parents, and tell my story. He sustains us, supplies comfort as we mourn, strengthens us when we're weak, and encourages us in times of fear. We may not know why we're going through something, but we know who to turn to: God Almighty, El Shaddai.

Prayer: *El Shaddai, we need Thee every hour. May our hope and trust be in You in every temptation, trial, and moment of joy. In Jesus' name, Amen.*

Journal Page — Day Fourteen

El Shaddai — The Lord is the All-Sufficient One

How priceless is your unfailing love, O God! People take refuge in the shadow of your wings. Psalm 36:7 (NIV)

1. Read the verse above aloud. Does anything stand out that you want to jot down about God?

2. Job is described as a righteous man who feared God and shunned evil. In your words, what does it mean to fear God?

3. What or whom have you depended on instead of God?

4. El Shaddai means all-sufficient. What, if any, comfort do you draw from the name?

5. Name as many words with the acrostic El Shaddai that relate to God's care of you:

E=
L=

S=
H=
A=
D=
D=
A=
I=

Additional Scriptures

But blessed is the one who trusts in the Lord, whose confidence is in him. Jeremiah 17:7 (NIV)

Day Fifteen

THE LORD IS — OUR TEACHER

On the second day of the month, the heads of all the families, along with the priests and the Levites, gathered around Ezra the teacher to give attention to the words of the Law. Nehemiah 8:13(NIV)

A recent experience led me to conclude that sometimes less is better. Also, our Father in Heaven has a delightful sense of humor. I'd scoured Zillow and Trulia websites for four years, searching for a smaller home. Health challenges and widowhood didn't play fair with inside home repairs, plus added outside chores to deal with. Thus, a place with less square footage seemed a logical solution, right? I'd prayed for God to guide me. He did, just not in the manner I expected.

My lesson occurred during a crucial subfloor repair. I knew I was in trouble when weariness set in just from transporting moving boxes into the house from the car. The next several days involved monotonous rounds of emptying and packing. Every shelf, chest, and cabinet was cleared for easier transport to an on-site storage unit. Packing and moving furniture from seven rooms took five days and five and six intermittent family volunteers. Muscles and joints ached in places I didn't know existed. A cold front blew in the morning, and floor workers commenced with constant sawing and hammering. Red dust, thick as fog coated surfaces. My nerves screamed and a sinus headache threatened to explode through my nostrils or head. Whose idea was this again?

The Babylonians destroyed the walls of Jerusalem and the temple. God utilized an exiled priest named Ezra for spiritual restoration and an exiled cupbearer turned governor named Nehemiah to reconstruct a wall, rebuild the city, and develop family leadership roles.

As governor, Nehemiah encouraged returning exiles to continue laboring despite intimidation, threats, and distractions from opposers. Three men joined forces in the name of evil to prevent the reconstruction. Good prevailed. Completion of the entire project succeeded in fifty-two days, just in time for the month of festivals.

On the first day of September, the month of a celebratory festival and embarking on a New Year, a repentant nation stood attentive to hear God's word taught. Ezra, positioned on a prepared high platform before them, was passionate about teaching the Word. The gracious hand of God, our master teacher, designed the scribe and priest with a desire to study, obey, and teach the law. He read the Torah. Everyone responsible enough to understand stood attentive and listened from dawn until midday. For six consecutive hours, people remained upright and gave heed because they discerned that the book represented God's Word.

Thirteen Levites and Nehemiah walked among the people and explained in more depth what Ezra recited so the people might gain absolute clarity. A tsunami season of life, such as the exile, taught the Israelites humility. Ezra blessed the Lord, the great God and teacher.

I'm thankful there are no age restrictions to study in life's classroom. One starlit evening after the workers left, I admired my home's finished floors and serene space. That was when an enlightenment of wisdom shone from Heaven. Home repair had led to my revitalization.

God wove profound truths in my heart during a mundane yet tricky process. First, He taught me to keep my mind, surroundings, and activities as uncluttered with junk as the spotless floors appeared. Next, I want to remain on the solid foundation of His laws, just as I stood on strong planking. Last, I want to appreciate what I have and know that less is more. When we placed furniture back in the house, guess who threw away and donated unnecessary items? The Lord used a practical, complex situation to teach and restore my spiritual insight.

Keep your eyes and ears open in the classroom. Do your best. Ask God to teach you to love as He loves. Trust that His lessons are always for your good. Study the guidebook of God the teacher.

Prayer: *Teach us to examine ourselves by the mirror of Your Word. Amen*

Journal Page — Day Fifteen

The Lord is — Our Teacher

On the second day of the month, the heads of all the families, along with the priests and the Levites, gathered around Ezra the teacher to give attention to the words of the Law. Nehemiah 8:13 (NIV)

1. Write down what comes to mind as you picture God, the teacher.

2. Do you focus on the sermon at church without being easily distracted? If not, list some ways that might help you focus.

3. List two people who have been instrumental teachers in your life.

4. Of the two above, did one introduce you to the Lord?

5. To whom are you teaching the Word of God?

6. In what ways are Christians ministers of God's abundant grace and mercy?

Additional Scripture

I am the Lord your God, who teaches you what is best for you and who directs you in the way you should go. Isaiah 48:17 (NIV)

Day Sixteen

JEHOVAH NACHAH — THE LORD IS OUR GUIDE

Your word is a lamp for my feet, a light on my path. Psalm 119:5 (NIV)

An editor's comment caused me to take a second look at a devotional, "The scripture story isn't the best one for this anecdote."

Search after search for the perfect verse only gained frustration until the hour's growing lateness bid me shut editing down. I clicked on the remote to watch mindless television while attending another chore. It powered on. The screen blacked out four times before I gave that up, also. Perplexed, I switched to reading Christian fiction. That was when the Lord showed out. On the second page, a character in distress yearned for guidance. She recalled her mother's favorite psalm and uttered the ideal text for my devotional. Amazing. The Lord directed my path and guided me to the exact scripture the story needed.

Psalm 119, the longest book in the Bible, promises blessings for those whose ways are blameless and who keep God's statutes and seek Him with all their hearts. It contains eight stanzas for each of the twenty-two Hebrew alphabet letters with the central theme being the Word of God. The fourteenth letter, Nun, pronounced noon, describes the Word as a lamp to the writer's feet and a light to his path. Right away, images of an oil lantern on a small wooden table, casting a wide circle of light and a tree-lined, winding pathway came to mind. The author trusted in the Lord and depended on His inspired laws. The lamp symbolizes darkness dispelled with light and affirms that the psalmist walked in faith.

Life's pathway may be marred by pebbles of suffering, storm clouds that rain down darkness and despair, or surprising curves, but the Lord who guides has promised to light the way with the wisdom of His statutes, commandments, and ordinances.

Both the Old and New Testaments have phenomenal assurances of God's guidance. He redirected my thoughts and plans with a single comment from an editor. Perhaps you're contemplating a decision. Seek direction from the Lord, who has your best interest in mind. He speaks through the Word to reveal clear, divine, and continual truth. Ask a prayer partner to pray with and for you. There's no chance of getting lost with God as our GPS.

Prayer: *We beseech the only wise God; please guide our path so we remain on the straight and narrow course to eternity with You. In Jesus' name. Amen.*

Journal Page — Day Sixteen

Jehovah Nachah-The Lord is Our Guide

Your word is a lamp for my feet, a light on my path. Psalm 119:5 (NIV)

1. What decisions are you challenged to seek God's guidance about?

2. How are most of your choices for relationships established? Major purchases? Life transitions?

3. Write an acrostic for direction with guidance:

G=
U=
I=
D=
A=
N=
C=
E=

Additional Scriptures

Guide me in your truth and teach me, for you are God my Savior, and my hope is in you all day long. Psalm 25:5 (NIV)

Day Seventeen

THE LORD IS — GOD WHO CHASTENS

Because the Lord disciplines the one he loves, and he chastens everyone he accepts as his son. Hebrews 12:6 (NIV)

How I hated for Big Mama to fetch a switch from a humongous elm tree in the field next to her house! Daddy's work belt packed more power on my skinny, brown legs. He had the nerve to say, "This is going to hurt me worse than it hurts you." As a child, that made no sense at all. That physical pain burned, but it didn't bruise my soul, like the gazes of disappointment the grown-ups cast my way for misbehaving. I think I'd rather have taken a beating than take the guilt trip. Our parents taught us an important lesson that followed into adulthood: Discipline corrects and prunes us into who we're purposed to be. The writer of Hebrews summed it up well in penning, "Whom the Lord loves He chastens."

Habakkuk, a faithful prophet whose name means wrestler, questioned the Lord: "How long? When will You chastise Your children for their blatant misbehavior?" This was after Judah disobeyed yet again. This time, they worshipped pagan idols and fellowshipped with foreigners.

God's ways are higher than ours. I visualized Habakkuk shaking his head in shock at God's less-than-satisfactory reply. Habakkuk questioned how the holy and just God could utilize the Chaldeans to punish His people. The wrestler contended with the Lord about that wicked nation, drunk with power, quick to violence, and prone to greed. From his sideline, earthly view, none of this made sense.

Like us today, the prophet forgot he cried out to the One who sits high yet knows all below. God didn't need Habakkuk's account of who did what to whom. Everyone who requires chastening will be dealt with in due time. The wicked Chaldeans would chastise Judah for their disobedience. Persia battled and conquered the arrogant Babylonians, aka Chaldeans, as just due for trusting in their power and wielding destruction against Israel. Chastening corrects, revamps, trains, and disciplines.

No correction is enjoyable, but sometimes, it is warranted to discipline us into soldiers of love, grace, and mercy on the battlefield for God. It generates character growth and produces thankfulness. Pray for

71

the Lord to help you transform adverse chastisements into an optimistic or practical tool for yourself and others. Remember, as God's child, you're chastened in love.

Prayer: *Thank You, Father, for adopting me as Your child and disciplining me in love. Amen.*

Journal Page — Day Seventeen

The Lord is God Who Chastens

Because the Lord disciplines the one he loves, and he chastens everyone he accepts as his son. Hebrews 12:6 (NIV)

1. When did the LORD chasten you? What growth resulted from the chastening?

2. Remember when you were disciplined as a child or an adult. How has our Creator used the circumstances for positivity in your life?

3. Do you believe discipline and punishment are the same thing? Explain?

4. How is correction by humans different from correction by God? How is it similar?

5. What emotional state were you in when you last chastened someone? What state should you be in? Explain

Additional Scriptures

Whoever heeds discipline shows the way to life, but whoever ignores correction leads others astray. Proverbs 10:17 (NIV)

Day Eighteen

JEHOVAH TIQVAH – THE LORD IS MY HOPE

For you have been my hope, O Sovereign LORD, my confidence since my youth. Psalm 71:5 (NIV)

In January, a new internet company dug up a rectangular patch of my yard to install underground cables. Where St. Augustine grass and a daffodil bed once flourished under Texas sunlight now lay a tract of dirt overlaid with unkempt hay. It grieved my heart to lose flowers my husband had planted before his illness and subsequent death. Now, I'd miss the spring blooms. Or so I thought until green shoots peeked above ground in February.

By the first of March, buds appeared. Determined daffodils had returned! In weeks to come, clusters of delicate white flowers unveiled themselves. Look at God. He'd nurtured and restored roots buried under the dirt. In the process, He'd kindled bright flames of hope. If God provided every nutrient for the grass of the fields, which were here one day and cut down the next, the sheer truth finally soaked in. I clasped my face in joy of the epiphany. Of course, He'd sustain and bring His beloved children through the dirt of burdens and cares. It's not always the big things.

Elijah looked for God in an earthquake and a fire, but the Lord appeared in a still, small voice. On my darkest days as a widow, and then when I lost a child to suicide, God showed up. He was in the swirling leaves of fall and sunrays peeking through pecan limbs, new growth on a houseplant, or an unexpected "just thinking of you" card in the mail. All these stirrings were gifts from God, our hope.

We will endure trials and trudge through valleys of hardship and pain. Our lives are like the grass of the field. We prevail despite weathering life storms like the fiery heat of sunrays, being thrashed to and fro by high winds, and being beaten by pelting cold rain or icy stones of hail. God is our hope. Press on. Eternity in Paradise awaits.

Study God's battle plan, which was written in the past, to teach us. The scriptures of witnesses who endured will encourage you to hold on to the hope of glory. He can fill you with all joy and peace as you trust Him. Persevere and wait like the determined daffodils.

Prayer: *Lord, my hope is built on You. Thank You for caring about every detail of our lives. Amen.*

Journal Page — Day Eighteen

Jehovah TiQvah — The Lord is My Hope

For you have been my hope, O Sovereign LORD, my confidence since my youth. Psalm 71:5 (NIV)

1. How has God been your hope?

2. What other scriptures give you a sense of hope? Have you memorized one of these?

3. Who can you share the hope of glory with?

4. What does "sovereign" mean?

5. What thoughts are foremost on your mind?

Additional Scriptures

Be joyful in hope, patient in affliction, faithful in prayer. Romans 12:12 (NIV)

Day Nineteen

YAHWEH – THE LORD IS THE LEADER OF LEADERS

The Lord will establish you as his holy people, as he promised you on oath if you keep the commands of the Lord your God and walk in his ways. Deuteronomy 28:9 (NIV)

On the evening of September 11, 2001, members of Congress joined other leaders on the Capitol steps in a powerful, public display of bipartisan unity. The night ended with a sobering rendition of *God Bless America*. Officials promised a nation staggering under the thick dust of grief, fear, anger, and disbelief that they would not forget. I prayed they would never forget. The horror might never leave survivors and family members who'd lost loved ones in the 2001 terrorist attack that cloaked our nation in sorrow. For a spell, they honored those words.

Asa, King of Judah, started his reign by eradicating Judah's pagan worship places and fencing the city for protection. Kingship conveyed from one generation to the next, so rulers weren't obligated to "sell their platform." Asa emulated his daddy, who declared to wicked Jeroboam of Israel, "The Lord is our God, and we have not forsaken him." Many of us can relate to our earliest church attendance and knowing that the love of God commenced with our parents and grandparents.

Judah's new king ordered the citizens to seek the Lord, who rescued their ancestors from Egyptian bondage. Yahweh still reigned. The I Am, who set captives free from Pharaoh and dried up a sea and river for safe passage to the Promised Land, didn't change.

A prophet delivered a conditional oath from God to Asa in his fifteenth year as Judah's ruler: "If you seek the Lord, He'll be found. If you forsake Him, He'll forsake you." (2 Chr. 15:12) Enough said. Asa trusted the One who'd battled his and his father's enemies. Every soul in Judah, whether male or female, including strangers, entered a covenant with God to seek Him or die. With that leadership, the land had peace for the next twenty years.

"Follow the Leader" was a popular playground game in my childhood. Imagine imitating the finger-pointing, divisive demeanor some current and hopeful political staff display publicly and on social media. Believers are invited and obligated to resemble our heavenly

Father in words and actions.

You and I can start by researching candidates to make informed voting choices. Consider running for local office. Vocally oppose injustice and write to current representatives. Speak the truth in love. Seek the Holy Spirit's guidance daily for discernment. The Word commands us to follow authority as it aligns with God's will. Visualize those who stated, "We shall never forget," joining hands again and beseeching, "Follow me as I follow Christ." Yahweh still reigns.

Prayer: *Father, You're the leader of leaders. Help us live in humble obedience. Grant us divine wisdom to elect officials who acknowledge You in all their ways. In Jesus's name. Amen.*

Journal Page — Day Nineteen

Yahweh — The Lord is the Leader of Leaders

The Lord will establish you as his holy people, as he promised you on oath, if you keep the commands of the Lord your God and walk in his ways. Deuteronomy 28:9 (NIV)

1. What does a promise from the Lord mean to you?

2. What qualities do you look for in a government official? A pastor and wife? Your employer?

3. Are these the same qualities you'd expect from your physician? Banker? Why or why not?

4. Who exemplified good leadership in your childhood?

5. Who should be the measuring standard to follow?

Additional Scriptures

For the Lord is our judge, the Lord is our lawgiver, the Lord is our king, it is he who will save us. Isaiah 33:22 (NIV)

Day Twenty

THE LORD IS — THE GOD OF REST

Then God blessed the seventh day and made it holy because on it he rested from all the work of creating that he had done. Genesis 2:3 (NIV)

I wheeled into the church parking lot by 8:47 a.m. and arrived home by noon. You'd think one would squeeze a nap in before afternoon choir practice, especially if an evening service followed. Instead of coming home and resting in between, a buzz of creativity tingled my fingers, and I worked. After I returned home from the 6:00 p.m. service, I wrote again until after 10:00 p.m. An elevated blood pressure reading on Monday morning reminded me that I should have received my blessing of rest yesterday. God declared a period to cease from labor. He led by example.

The Lord created the world in six days and pronounced all He had made as good. He chose not to work on the seventh day and set it apart as a day of restoration. Our bodies require sleep, sustenance, and hydration to thrive. Working excessive hours without a day off will cause exhaustion and other health problems. One who habitually rises too early and stays up too late accomplishes as much as a hamster on a spinning wheel. Nothing. When rested, creativity and purpose are maximized.

A high blood pressure reading frightened me into going to bed earlier the next night. Don't wait for dire vital readings. Be proactive. Consider carving in a short daily nap time. Pray and seek God's guidance as you implement a schedule to incorporate rest periods. Give thanks to the One who ordained a day of rest.

Prayer: *Father, when our eyes are gritty and our minds foggy with weariness, we thank You for the gift of rest. In Jesus' name, Amen.*

Journal Page — Day Twenty

The Lord is — The God of Rest

Then God blessed the seventh day and made it holy, because on it he rested from all the work of creating that he had done. Genesis 2:3 (NIV)

1. How many days and hours a week do you work?

2. Write down the first image that comes to mind when you say, "Day of rest."

3. Describe what your dream day of rest would look like.

4. Have you ever experienced fatigue from working too much? What were the consequences? What decisions were made to overcome the problem?

5. What do you imagine are some physical, mental, or emotional concerns you might suffer from lack of rest in the future? How will that impact those around you?

Additional Scriptures

In peace I will lie down and sleep, for you alone, Lord, make me dwell in safety. Psalm 4:8 (NIV)

Day Twenty-One

Two-Part Series on Breaking the Bondage of Fear
PART 1: THE LORD IS — THE GOD WHO ALLAYS MY FEARS

So do not fear, for I am with you. Do not be dismayed, for I am your God.
Isaiah 41:10a (NIV)

The noise of lawn chairs on the back porch being shuffled and banged against the house startled me. I glanced out the kitchen window and viewed my pear and pecan trees twisting and swaying in high winds. Huge limbs thrashed and bowed like dancers in a frantic ballet. The overcast sky outside and the noticeable lack of light inside indicated the storm meteorologists predicted might arrive earlier than expected.

My phone pinged. A friend requested prayer. "Please pray for our house and tree. I'm afraid of what the storm may do." The massive tree was rooted dangerously close to their beautiful farm-style home. They'd secured bids to trim it months ago, but local contractors were weeks behind. I typed back a quick prayer, then obeyed a strong urge to call. After the first ring, she picked up, "All I can think about is what if that tree falls. I wasn't concerned until people talked about how bad the storms would be. Those folks had me ready to buy a saw and tackle that massive giant." We both laughed.

She thanked me for not judging her fear. I'm grateful believers don't have to hide behind masks of pretense. We can admit our fears and solicit prayers from other believers. Fright from the flesh remains a battle until we go to heaven. God does not give us a spirit of fear. We inherited that trait from our first forefather, Adam. He hid in the Garden of Eden. Why? The first man panicked, thinking God would discover his nakedness. The cure for fear is a fixed gaze on the One who allays our fears.

The Israelites endured seventy years of extradition by the Babylonian ruler, Nebuchadnezzar. Now, God's chosen waited. Cyrus of Persia conquered the Babylonians. Would he hand out afflictions and oppressions like his predecessor? Isaiah chapters 40-41 communicated a love letter from a dear Father. They're intended to ease the mind and unburden the hearts of His children despite their past actions. God reassured the Israelites of His divine power and choice to stir up a ruler who would release them, and His omnipresence with every generation. His instructions in the verse above, "Do not fear," echoed like a parent's summation of a message of encouragement, replete with a tissue: "Here, wipe your nose. Everything will be okay."

A wealth of peace enveloped me as I beseeched the Father on my friend's behalf. An audible sigh echoed through the phone receiver. When we declared our belief and pleaded for help with our weaknesses, I sensed His strength infused her. God knows all. Let's shed pretense. Run to Him naked of pride and ask in child-like faith. Storms may come, and trees could fall, but God is greater than any terror. He who stills the winds and quiets thunderous nights will calm your angst and remove all fright.

Prayer: *Father, thank You for hearing my call. Thank You for loving us one and all. Thank You. Fear has no hold on me when I'm in Your hands. In Jesus' name, Amen.*

Journal Page — Day Twenty-One

Part 1: The Lord is — The God Who Allays Our Fears

So do not fear, for I am with you. Do not be dismayed, for I am your God.
Isaiah 41:10a (NIV)

1. The Israelites brought the Babylonian captivity and other punishments on themselves because they ignored God and disobeyed Him. They should have feared Him. Do you have a healthy fear of the Lord?

2. How would you define fear?

3. Who were the Israelites afraid of, as referenced in the devotion?

4. Look at the verse above. Can you recognize another name of God in each of the two sentences?

5. Change FEAR into a win by naming something positive to do for each letter of the word:

F=
E=
A=
R=

Additional Scriptures

I sought the Lord, and he answered me. He delivered me from all my fears.
Psalm 34:4 (NIV)

Day Twenty-Two

Two-Part Series on Breaking the Bondage of Fear
Part 2: THE LORD IS – OUR GOD IN THE DAY OF FEAR

You came near when I called you, and you said, "Do not fear."
Lamentations 3:57 (NIV)

An adolescent trudged by me in the parking lot of a local superstore. His hands were cupped in loose fists, and his face scrunched in a scowl instead of a smile. I noted the red No Fear emblazoned across the front of his t-shirt. Maybe that was the image he endeavored to portray. Were intense body language and posture mere props to prove bravery, while inside tentacles of fear gripped him?

Adults also experience fear. I knew the terror of my auto headed straight for oncoming traffic after someone rammed me from behind. There was nowhere to go. My chest tightened as car lights zoomed closer. God sent angels or directed movement from heaven. Someone other than me wove that crew cab truck amidst approaching traffic within inches of a steel electrical box to go off-road. It mowed down brush and rested in a live power line and thicket of trees.

Jeremiah, known as the Weeping Prophet, spoke of despair, but I wondered if he swallowed lumps of fear to declare, "Thus saith the Lord…"

Lamentations 3:55-57 reference when the prophet was thrown into a waterless dungeon by princes of Judah's king and sank in the mire. The men accused him of sabotaging their army and working for the Babylonians. Imagine Jeremiah, a regular man who spoke what God told him to say, as he was lowered by rope into a hole underneath the home of the king's son. Did dread increase his heart rate? Perhaps he struggled to breathe in the pitch black and wrestled to remain calm. Dungeons are dark and airless. Mire is defined as wet, spongy earth or heavy, deep mud. For sure, the spokesperson remembered who to call on. He cried out, "O Lord." God heard and answered.

Although defensive body language may be helpful in the right surroundings, it can't help us tackle fear. The initial angst that materialized when I knew the other vehicle would hit me evaporated. The moment God controlled the situation, peace reigned. Panicked? Intimidated by new surroundings? Threatened by an unknown future? Like Jeremiah, cry to the Lord who draws near in your days of fear.

Prayer: *O Lord, thank You for drawing near in days of fear. I will trust in you. In Jesus' name. Amen.*

Journal Page — Day Twenty-Two

Part 2: The Lord is — Our God in A Day of Fear

You came near when I called you, and you said, "Do not fear." Lamentations 3:57 (NIV)

1. Define fear.

2. How can lamenting help your faith?

3. What part of your spiritual life is mired?

4. List characteristics that might suggest one is in a spiritual dungeon.

Additional Scriptures

The LORD is my light and my salvation — whom shall I fear? Psalm 27:1 (NIV)

Day Twenty-Three

EL EMUNAH – THE LORD IS OUR FAITHFUL GOD

Know therefore that the Lord your God is God; he is the faithful God, keeping his covenant of love to a thousand generations of those who love him and keep his commandments. Deuteronomy 7:9 (NIV)

Two days past Thanksgiving, I palmed a Christmas ornament designed with a picture of my deceased son and marveled at how far God had brought me. Days later, tears of joy trickled as my fingers flicked across a laptop keyboard. I paused to wrist them away, sniffled, and continued. Hidden potholes, valleys, and detours plagued my life's journey. He pulled me through the scorching flames of gossip and shame as I suffered through adultery and the deep waters of grief after a son's suicide.

Our God perched me on a front-row seat to witness the transformation of my spouse to a new creation in Christ and a vocal testimony of the Lord's saving power. God's Word comforted and renewed my purpose when my husband graduated to heaven. The same faithful I Am spared my life in an auto accident. Spiritual maturity has blessed me and allowed me to understand that my faithful God always had a plan.

Deborah judged Israel and testified of God's faithfulness. She and Barak sang an impromptu song of praise because they understood who delivered the nation from the Canaanites.

Judges record a proverbial song of behavior for God's people. Repeated disobedience resulted in swift consequences. At once, they begged God for mercy. God responded by sending a rescuer. This time He called Deborah, a wife, mother, and prophet. The Lord charged her to commission Barak, whose name ironically means lightning, to lead the people against the enemy. Barak's reluctance to take charge alone forced Deborah to co-lead. Ten thousand more men aligned with their army because of the dynamic duo, plus help arrived from other tribes. The Lord fought for them. Deborah and Barak magnified and honored the Lord in unrestrained worship and thanks. His faithful guidance led them to victory.

My hardships produced the characteristics listed above. God has run my cup over with good. How dare I keep it to myself? What a privilege to use video, written, and vocal testimonies to spread the marvelous news of His steadfast care.

Life without trials and sorrow is impossible on earth. Lean and depend on God. Recall how He has brought you through before. There's also a great cloud of witnesses in the Word. You may know someone whom God has carried through the darkness. Think about their testimony and the promise that God is no respecter of persons. Ask the Lord to open your eyes to opportunities to encourage others by telling your story.

Prayer: *Because of who You are we have come this far by faith. Thank You for blessing us to trust in Your Word. In Jesus' name, Amen.*

Journal Page — Day Twenty-Three

El Emunah — The Lord is Our Faithful God

Know therefore that the Lord your God is God; he is the faithful God, keeping his covenant of love to a thousand generations of those who love him and keep his commandments. Deuteronomy 7:9 (NIV)

1. What is a covenant in your words?

2. What is the minimum number of people required for a covenant?

3. What is a commandment?

4. Where have you witnessed God's faithfulness in a unique way?

5. Are you seeking God's faithfulness for a particular situation?

Additional Scriptures

A faithful God who does no wrong, upright, and just is he. Deuteronomy 32:4 (NIV)

Day Twenty-Four

EL NOE' — THE LORD IS THE FORGIVING GOD

O Lord our God, you answered them. You were to Israel a forgiving God, though you punished their misdeeds. Psalm 99:8 (NIV)

I associated Celebrate Recovery with programs for drug addicts and alcoholics until I spoke with someone involved in the ministry. Her transparency drew me to listen. Cheryl, a new facilitator, seemed sincere and passionate about helping others. It echoed in her firm belief that C.R.'s steps and principles worked because they were based on God's Word. My interest was piqued when Cheryl talked about hurts, hang-ups, habits, and how people hurt others in words and actions if they have not healed. She extended an invitation that changed my life: "We're having an informational gathering next Tuesday. Why don't you come?"

Attendance at the meeting helped me understand that participants of Celebrate Recovery use the Bible as the primary textbook. The program is for everyone struggling to overcome hurts, habits, or hangups. It's a worldwide ministry supported by a local church. Members' success depends on doing the work, which includes evaluating all relationships and creating a written inventory of those to whom we owe amends. Next, act. Amends is defined as making up for wrongdoing. We must also forgive others who have offended or hurt us.

The time spent contemplating pain had as much appeal as an abscessed tooth—none. However, the marked differences in this process included an influx of scripture to meditate on and apply at each step of self-examination and confession. No matter how badly I sensed past mistakes in judgment, viewing them through God's grace and mercy enabled me to forgive myself. Accepting His forgiveness compelled me to release resentment and anger against persons and institutions. The Bible records stories of people who hurt one another and possessed hangups.

Joseph, son of Jacob, dreamed about an influential future in which his parents and brothers would one day bow down before him. Jacob had twelve sons. He loved each one yet favored Joseph. God has innumerable children. He doesn't deem one more important than another. Each is created with talent and plans. Joseph's purpose caused him pain and triumph.

The Dreamer, so named by his siblings because of the visions he shared with his family, endured afflictions such as betrayal by his brothers, being sold as a slave, being lied to, and being locked up in jail for years. The Lord's hand lay steadfast on Jacob's son.

One day, Pharoah desired someone to interpret his strange night visions. No one could do it but Joseph. His status transformed from prisoner to Egypt's second-in-command. Infused with godly wisdom, Joseph instituted a program to amass food in the predicted seven years of plenty because famine followed in the next seven years.

His brothers arrived in Egypt during the famine and sought food from the commander. They didn't recognize their brother. Joseph knew, comforted, and forgave his brothers: "Don't be grieved. You sold me with bad intent, but God ordered a plan."

I celebrate life and how God has used the ugly ashes of naivete, lack of self-worth, and betrayal as tools of encouragement to others. Sincere sorrow for words and actions that might cause others hurt compels me to say and mean, "I'm sorry." Forgiveness frees the one chained to bitterness, anger, or resentment. Every time I study a Celebrate Recovery lesson, I'm struck by how much God has forgiven me. How dare I hold anything against anyone else? Ask God to aid you or someone you care about to forgive. Search for all the scriptures on forgiving in the Bible. Write them in a journal. Read over them daily. Be a conduit of healing for others having difficulty forgiving by sharing what you have learned.

Prayer: *God, please forgive me for my sins against You and others. Help me to forgive as You forgive me. Amen.*

Journal Page—Day Twenty-Four

El Noe'—The Lord is the Forgiving God

O Lord our God, you answered them. You were to Israel a forgiving God, though You punished their misdeeds. Psalm 99:8 (NIV)

Reflection: The writer of this Psalm is unknown. The words above inspire us to note that the Holy God 1) answered prayers, 2) forgave the offenders—Israel, and 3) charged consequences for their disobedience.

1. Is forgiving someone the same as overlooking the offense? Support your answer.

2. Which one is easier to forgive? A stranger or a loved one? Why?

3. Have you experienced the Lord's forgiveness in an extraordinary sense?

4. Is there someone God is calling you to forgive? Have you ever had to forgive yourself?

Additional Scriptures

Be kind and compassionate to one another, forgiving each other, just as in Christ God forgave you. Ephesians 4:32 (NIV)

Day Twenty-Five

THE LORD IS – GOD WHO HEALS

Go back and tell Hezekiah, the ruler of my people, 'This is what the Lord, the God of your father David, says: I have heard your prayer and seen your tears; I will heal you. On the third day from now you will go up to the temple of the Lord." 2 Kings 20:5 (NIV)

This devotion occurred when news came across our church thread on the Messenger app. A dear brother in Christ's health had deteriorated. He required emergency surgery. I prayed for healing and texted a prayer to encourage his wife and son before continuing to work. My phone continued to ping notifications. Petitions from our forever family united in one accord via social media in fervent appeal for Darrell's healing.

King Hezekiah fell ill and was near death, so he petitioned God, too. He reigned over the southern kingdom of Judah starting at age twenty-five. The king depended on God and gleaned spiritual wisdom from Isaiah, the prophet. His first orders of business in office included ridding the temple and town of pagan places of worship, reopening the temple in Jerusalem, and reinstating the Levitical priesthood.

National reformation thrived in Judah after the reinstitution of the Passover. King Hezekiah sought the Lord first in all he took to task. When Isaiah prophesied, "You're going to die," the king stayed true to form.

"Lord, remember now how I have conducted myself in truth with a pure heart and what was good in Your sight." He wept hard.

The One who heals heard. Before Isaiah could exit the palace, God answered, "You will be healed."

Darrell's surgery proved successful. Again, Messenger notifications chimed one after another, this time with praise and thanks. If you or someone you care about seeks a cure, pray God's promises back to Him. Trust the Lord who heals on earth and in heaven.

Prayer: *Heal us, Lord and we shall be healed. We trust you in all things. Amen.*

Journal Page — Day Twenty-Five

The Lord is — God Who Heals

Go back and tell Hezekiah, the ruler of my people, 'This is what the Lord, the God of your father David, says: I have heard your prayer and seen your tears; I will heal you. On the third day from now you will go up to the temple of the Lord." 2 Kings 20:5 (NIV)

1. Have you experienced a waiting period to hear news of a loved one in surgery? What thoughts ran through your mind? How did you spend the time?

2. Do you believe the same God who heard Hezekiah hears your prayers? Why or why not?
   Cross-reference Hebrews 13:8

3. God stated He heard and saw Hezekiah. Does this give you comfort? How so?

4. Who are you praying for in this season for healing?

5. What does it mean to be absent from the body but present with the Lord?

Additional Scriptures

Heal me, Lord, and I will be healed. Jeremiah 17:14 (NIV)

Day Twenty-Six

ELOHEI TEHILLATI – THE LORD IS GOD OF MY PRAISE

O God, whom I praise. Psalm 109:1a (NIV)

At the end of choir practice, I chose a private moment to ask our music director a question. "Should I be less demonstrative?" His warm smile put me at ease.

"Sharon, you can't please everybody. Be yourself."

How could I subdue praise to our deserving God for His goodness and mercy? Song lyrics prompted total focus and remembrance of what the Lord had done for me – a symphony of rich music-enhanced worship. Psalm 150 urges every living being to praise the Lord with various instruments. King David learned that our Holy God desires everything in reverential order.

Michal burned with wrath because her husband, King David, leaped about and danced in the street as the Ark of the Covenant returned to Jerusalem. She considered his behavior and clothing improper for a king. David cast aside her rebuke. He praised God in a sincere, energetic manner. The Lord blessed them with the return of the Ark that represented His presence, and He'd chosen a former shepherd boy as leader over His people. "I will be undignified and humiliated to celebrate the Lord," David declared to Michal. (2 Sam. 6:22)

I close my eyes sometimes while our choir leads worship. It allows me to feel like I'm singing to an audience of one: God. Be sincere. He commands decency and order and knows our hearts. Exercise those vocal cords throughout the week. They're not restricted just to Sabbath use. Let creation and circumstances prompt spontaneous songs. The Lord is worthy to be praised.

Prayer: *Father, I praise You for who You are. In Jesus' name, Amen.*

Journal Page — Day 26

The Lord is — God of My Praise

O God, Whom I Praise. Psalm 109:1 (NIV)

Reflection: Praising God isn't a spectator event. It's heartfelt participation.

1. What is your preferred way to worship?

2. How do you display praise to God?

3. Solomon's quiet-mannered services are said to show reverence, deep respect, and love for God. How does that differ from making "a joyful noise to the Lord" in Psalm 100? Are both deemed appropriate methods of service?

4. What or who determines if praise and worship are appropriate?

Additional Scriptures

Let everything that has breath praise the Lord. Praise the Lord. Psalm 150:6 (NIV)

Day Twenty-Seven

EL KHAYYAI—THE LORD IS THE GOD OF MY LIFE

By day the LORD directs his love, at night his song is with me — a prayer to the God of my life. Psalm 42:8 (NIV)

The Bible illustrates friendship between God and man, between humanity and their pets. At the root of these relationships is love and respect. You love your friend as you love yourself. My friendship with MJ has endured the test of time and distance. Late one night, she occupied my mind and heart. Something pushed me to call and check on her. The phone rang twice before she picked up. "Hello? Are you okay?" Silence "Umm…you were on my heart. Is everything all right?" Regret stabbed deep in my navel. I didn't know it yet, but the Lord of my life worked even though I couldn't see it.

"Girl, it's late. Get some rest. We'll talk later."

MJ hung up before I replied. That wasn't like her at all.

God called two men around the same time to preach the gospel to the Gentiles. They also exhibited out of the norm behavior. Paul, a well-to-do Roman citizen, worked as a tentmaker. Barnabas, a Levite from Cyprus owned real estate. Both preached and taught the Lord's Word in Antioch. They made plans to revisit all the previous cities and check on the people. Conflict transpired when Barnabas wanted to invite his cousin John Mark to join them. Paul disagreed since John Mark left them during work on a previous missionary journey.

An intense disagreement pulled the duo apart. Separation seemed unfortunate at first, however the Lord of our lives turned a negative into a positive. Paul took Silas to Syria and Cilicia. Barnabas and John Mark sailed to Cyprus. Mark continued to work faithfully under Barnabas' tutelage. From observing his and Barnabas' fellowship, Paul gained respect for John Mark's growth and wisdom. He then took on a protégé named Timothy. Paul and Barnabas reconciled. Two young men gained unparalleled mentorships, and the church profited.

I'm amazed at how God nudges me to phone, text, or drop by a friend or family member's home. MJ phoned two days later. She shared how a beloved family member had blindsided her with a vicious verbal attack just before I phoned.

"It didn't make sense. I couldn't process what happened in my mind. How could I explain it to anyone else?"

Though shock and hurt at first bound my friend, God used my call to remind her He is ever present. Come what may, night or day, the God of life works behind the scenes and directs our path.

I've learned that words aren't always necessary to obey the Lord's guidance. Your presence and love mean much. While listening, a hug, nod, or smile is worth more than silver. Trust God. Obey even when you don't understand. We ended our conversation in prayer. The crisis hasn't been resolved, yet my friend's steadfast hope realigned with the God of our lives. Pray daily for wisdom to walk in His will.

Prayer: *God of my life, may I trust You as you add or remove people, places, or things. In Jesus's name, Amen.*

Journal Page — Day Twenty-Seven

The Lord is — The God of My Life

By day the LORD directs his love, at night his song is with me — a prayer to the God of my life. Psalm 42:8 (NIV)

1. Does the verse above give you comfort? Any particular part?

2. Do you trust all your life to God? If not, what part are you trying to control?

3. What will it take to give Him all of it? I'm working on this one — addiction to sugary foods.

4. What actions do you sense the Lord directing you to take after studying this devotion?

5. Prayers and concerns:

Additional Scriptures

There is a time for everything, and a season for every activity under the heavens. Ecclesiastes 3:1 (NIV)

Day Twenty-Eight

EL-NEQAMOT – THE LORD IS THE GOD OF VENGEANCE

It is mine to avenge; I will repay. In due time their foot will slip. Their day of disaster is near and their doom rushes upon them. Deuteronomy 32:35 NIV

My chest burned. A stream of anger seemed to rocket off like a missile and explode inside my head. Helpless frustration and sadness mounted as I continued to view a horrific scene on TV. How does a man remain so unaffected while kneeling on the neck of another human being? Lord help! I can't believe this is happening! Make him get off that man. Somebody ought to do that to him.

The Holy Spirit spoke through my conscience. Hearing, "God will take care of it," I sighed in remorse. Tension deflated, taut shoulders relaxed as I relented. "Forgive me, Father. May Your will be done." We should care about and act against such injustices in our world. Our righteous anger should not, however, lead us to sin.

Fueled by self-righteous rage because Ishbosheth, Saul's son, accused him of sleeping with the king's concubine, Abner, former commander of the royal troops allied with King David. Abner threatened Ishbosheth, "I will transfer the kingdom from the house of Saul and establish David's throne over Israel and Judah." (2 Sam.3:10)

Abner wasn't the only angry one in the story who plotted vengeance. Joab, leader of David's troops, secretly sent for Abner and stabbed him under the fifth rib for killing his brother. When David received news of the cold-blooded killing, he denounced guilt in his kingdom. Joab and his family were cursed with illness, hunger, life as lepers, or death by the sword forever. Abner's quest for vengeance eventually led to loss of life. Joab's burning desire for revenge cost every member of his household for all generations, including those already born and those in the future.

The Holy Spirit pricked my conscience for wanting another human to act as an avenger. Remorse deflated tension-taut shoulders. Sorrow for the victim, his family, and onlookers who cried out to stop the inhumane crime remained. Righteous indignation channeled into lawful actions, blessed by God, will yield results. Prayer rallies, letters to elected officials, and peaceful protests are examples.

Our Righteous Judge will avenge the wronged. Continue to pray for victims and offenders. Pray that the light of God's love will penetrate the darkness that energizes evil actions. Grow a garden of kindness in your circle of influence. We should care about and act against such injustices in our world. So don't let righteous anger lead to sin.

Emotions are difficult to subdue in high-profile criminal cases where severe trauma or death occurs. We can stay grounded by remembering our true identity as children of God. It trumps race, geographical, financial, socio-economical, and religious preferences.

Prayer: *Help us, Father, to choose right in a world where we witness so much wrong. We believe in You. In Jesus' name, Amen.*

Journal Page — Day Twenty-Eight

The Lord is — The God of Vengeance

The Lord is a God who avenges. O God who avenges, shine forth. Psalm 94:1 (NIV)

1. Have you ever attempted to repay someone for causing harm? If yes, was it worth it?

2. List reasons why God should be the avenger and not man.

3. Would you choose forgiving over exacting revenge? Why or why not?

Additional Scriptures

It is mine to avenge; I will repay. In due time their foot will slip. Their day of disaster is near, and their doom rushes upon them. Deuteronomy 32:35 NIV

Day Twenty-Nine

THE LORD IS — GOD WHO KNOWS ME BY NAME

And the Lord said to Moses, I will do the very thing you have asked, because I am pleased with you, and I know you by name. Exodus 33:17 (NIV)

Two weeks before Thanksgiving, I spotted an estranged relative in a busy department store. He sat fifteen feet from where I stood in a checkout line. An urge filled me to run over, give him a big hug, and shout, "I love and miss you all." Do it.

I rushed through self-check-out before my courage evaporated. He'd cast the sweetest smile toward a customer before me. No sooner had our gazes met than he glared and drew away. Hurt coiled in my core for a loved one to treat me like a leper. Raised brows of nearby shoppers led me to wheel my shopping cart around in shame and race toward the nearest exit. Outside the store, I hurried across the parking lot to my vehicle. It transformed into a sanctuary where I cried out to God. The God who knows my name met me there. He dried unshed tears and scabbed a fresh sore.

God commanded Moses to lead a stiff-necked people to the Promised Land, but Moses wanted assurance of His presence with them: "You have said that You know me by name, and You're pleased with me. I want to know and find favor with You." The leader then reminded God to whom the Israelites belonged and added, "Don't send us without Your presence." God guaranteed He would do as Moses asked because the trailblazer pleased Him, and affirmed He knew him by name. The Lord also blessed Aaron and Miriam's brother to view His glory from the cleft of a rock.

Quiet time in God's presence refreshed my countenance. His Word reminded me that I'm loved, and He engraved my name on His palm. You may encounter rejection from people, a place of employment, or a financial institution. Please remember that others' opinions don't determine your identity or success. Spend quality and quantity time in the presence of the One who knows you by name. Seek to learn all you can to know Him better.

Prayer: *God of wonder, thank You for knowing my name and history yet offering agape love. I worship You. In Jesus' name, Amen.*

Journal Page — Day Twenty-Nine

The Lord is — God Who Knows Me by Name

And the Lord said to Moses, I will do the very thing you have asked, because I am pleased with you, and I know you by name. Exodus 33:17 (NIV)

1. What does it mean to you when a store clerk or waiter remembers your name?

2. How important is it that the One who created the world knows your name?

3. Have you suffered rejection? What were the circumstances?

4. What is your favorite name for God? Why?

Additional Scriptures

But now, this is what the LORD says — he who created you, Jacob, he who formed you, Israel: Do not fear, for I have redeemed you; I have summoned you by name; you are mine. Isaiah 43:1 (NIV)

Day Thirty

JEHOVAH NASA – THE LORD IS GOD WHO LIFTS MY SINS OFF

For I know my transgressions, and my sin is always before me. Psalm 51:3 (NIV)

Sunday morning, I itched to share words on social media ASAP. That eagerness compelled me to rush ahead with a project and neglect steps. I intended to film and download the video before time to leave for church. Even though I'd read the scripture chosen numerous times, it's best to proofread before posting. I'm accountable to God for the words I share, whether via social media, book form, or vocal.

That evening, I perused the section for audience participation in the hope that the message would resonate with others. Sixty-three people had viewed it. That was when a typographical error stood out. It's the right title but the wrong scripture verse. Several attempts to edit proved in vain. With each failed attempt, the room grew warmer, and a gnawing ache in my stomach intensified. *Lord, help. I'm sorry.* He blessed me with the wisdom to delete and start over. *Thank You, Father.* I can empathize with David's plea for forgiveness.

Psalm 51 stands as a solemn reminder that any wrongdoing is against God. King David's anger burned when the prophet Nathan informed him of a gross miscarriage of justice. A rich man took the only ewe a poor man owned to feed a stranger. David responded, "The wealthy guy's actions were unjust because he owned a whole herd of sheep. The offender's punishment should be quick and severe." Imagine the king's guilt and shame as Nathan declared, "It's you. God delivered you from Saul and made you king. Uriah had one wife. You sent him to the front line of battle and had him murdered to cover sin."

"I have sinned before God," David confessed and repented.

Conscious decisions affect us and those in our circle with long-range consequences. Every sin committed is against our Holy God. Pause, think, and pray before making decisions. David should have assembled with the other kings and not lounged on the rooftop. Be at the right place at the right time. I could have tempered my excitement and posted the video after church. Instead, I spent anxious hours on Sunday night correcting a mess. King David made a conscious decision to take something not his

117

own. God commanded us not to steal or kill. His actions caused heartache to an innocent family.

I've learned to ask God daily to guide my footsteps and order my tongue in His Word. Starting the day off with Bible study and prayer keeps one's focus centered on God. We're less apt to fall to the temptation of the flesh, enemy, and the world. If failure does occur, confess it right away. Pray for strength not to repeat the same mistake. Write, "all sin is against God," on a slip of paper, and place it in a prominent spot as a reminder. I'm grateful God blessed me with the wisdom to delete and start over. Thank You, Father.

Prayer: *Forgive me, Father, for where I have failed You in sins of commission and omission. My heart desires to please You. In Jesus' name, Amen.*

Journal Page—Day Thirty

The Lord is—God Who Lifts My Sins Off

For I know my transgressions, and my sin is always before me. Psalm 51:3 (NIV)

1. Has a split-second decision you made caused negative consequences?

2. How can you help others avoid the pitfall?

3. Write words that describe the effects of sin:

S=
I=
N=
S=

4. How would you approach your supervisor to tell them they have mistreated another?

5. When did you last confess a sin? Did you seek forgiveness?

Additional Scriptures

If we confess our sins, he is faithful and just and will forgive us our sins and purify us from all unrighteousness. 1 John 1:9 (NIV)

Day Thirty-One

THE LORD IS — GOD WHO HAS ALL THE ANSWERS

And who knows but that you have come to your royal position for such a time as this? Esther 4:14b (NIV)

"What do I do?" I lamented to the perplexed gray-haired woman peering back at me from the bathroom mirror. Holidays ring in a mixture of joy for the season with angst and the pressure of coordinating with whom or where we spend our time. As the family unit increases or decreases via marriage, childbirth, divorce, death, or estrangement, it becomes more difficult to gather in one central place for Thanksgiving or Christmas.

With the addition of two great-grandchildren, I longed to gather my kids and grandchildren under one roof *and* spend time with Mama and my siblings. You might say, "Just spend time with both." That would work if we lived closer, but travel time between my house and my brother's spanned almost four hours. Hence, I stood at the mirror and sought advice from my reflection. Then a thought transpired: "Ask the Lord. He has the answer."

Queen Esther found herself in a precarious position due to a wicked scheme. An official of the palace plotted to destroy the Jewish people. Esther's cousin, Mordecai, pleaded with her to speak with the king immediately. The young woman had followed her wise cousin's advice without exception. He'd stepped up as guardian since her parents' deaths, but now Mordecai demanded she stroll into King Xerxes' throne room uninvited. That bit of counsel spelled a death sentence, even for a wife, if the king didn't signal for her. What should Esther do? Should she follow her cousin's advice without question or ignore him? She sent word back, "He hasn't called for me in thirty days."

Mordecai's sharp retort didn't mince words. "You're still a Jew. Don't think the Xerxes house will save you. Who knows whether you were placed in the kingdom for such a time as this?"

Esther heeded the reply and turned to the One with all the answers. She sent word requesting all the Jews fast for three days and nights. Queen Esther acted in faith, confident that God would supply answers.

We should opt for prayer as our first choice when making decisions.

It would trim quite a bit of useless worrying. God answered through a timely conversation with a granddaughter. She strolled into the kitchen with a huge grin. "I'm so excited that we're hosting Christmas, Granny."

"I'm torn between staying here and going out of town with Mama," I sighed and continued to voice concerns. Mya listened and nodded without interrupting as I spoke, nodding her head now and then.

Mya's soft reply resonated. "It sounds like you want to stay home, Granny," she remarked as I paused. "Grandma will understand. She'll remember her first great-grandchildren's Christmas."

Her wise, practical words were just what I needed. The next generation deserves to learn about the true meaning of Christmas and family traditions at grandma's house. I chose to host my children and grands for Christmas. Remember that we may devise ideas, but God orders our steps. I'd advise you to trust the Lord, who has all the answers. Embrace His will with a thankful and humble heart. Remember, everyone and everything we claim as ours belongs to Him.

Prayer: *Thank You, Father, for the holiday season. May we seek You for every answer needed. Help us be mindful not to get so caught up in plans that we waste precious time that should be spent worshiping and adoring You. In Jesus' name, Amen.*

Journal Page—Day Thirty-One

The Lord Is—God Who Has All the Answers

And who knows but that you have come to your royal position for such a time as this? Esther 4:14b (NIV)

1. Explain how the job, housing location, or school you attend may be divinely appointed for today.

2. Have you stood at the crossroads of indecision and frustration? How did you manage it?

3. Do you seek God for answers in every area of life, or is there a section marked, 'private'?

4. Name two godly people God has placed in your life who will speak the truth in love as Mordecai did with Esther.

Additional Scriptures

Trust in the Lord with all your heart and lean not on your own understanding; in all your ways submit to him, and he will make your paths straight. Proverbs 3:5-6 (NIV)

Day Thirty-Two

THE LORD IS — IMMUTABLE

I the Lord do not change. So, you, the descendants of Jacob, are not destroyed.
Malachi 3:6 (NIV)

Yesterday, the sun shone bright, and the temperature fell to 39 degrees. Today, it's balmy and warm. East Texas weather has earned a rightful reputation for its variation of temperatures in a short period. Some have quipped, "If you don't like the weather, stick around. It will change soon." One thing we trust in that has never failed is God's immutability. He's the same today as yesterday and will be forever.

Life changed drastically for a prophet of God named Elijah. He plunged from a mountaintop spiritual victory at Carmel and landed bereft in a valley of testing. Queen Jezebel threatened to kill Elijah the same way he'd slain her husband's 450 prophets on the mountain. Elijah ran for his life.

Imagine this ordinary man, adrenaline pumping, driven by fear and determination, sprinting to the top of a mountain to search for rain. Experience-sore and tired muscles strained as Elijah pounded back down the rugged mountain and ran seventeen miles to meet King Ahab in Jezreel. All of this after he'd dealt with the king's Baal worshippers.

Even in the wilderness, God continued to take care of Elijah. God remained a secure, unchanged anchor by fulfilling the prophet's every need in impossible situations. Ravens brought him bread and meat in the morning. Even though drought caused water shortage, a nearby brook provided water. After the brook dried, the Lord dispatched Elijah to a penniless widow who supplied sustenance. No matter what stomach-dropping, unexpected changes Elijah encountered, God stayed steadfast. The immutable God is our changeless hope and stay.

I've learned to dress in layers and carry an umbrella. The morning could be clear and freezing, raining by noon, and in the low 60s at the end of a workday. An adaptable attitude to life's unpredictable storms can be attained. Focus on the never-changing, divine forecaster. He created you. Encourage yourself with the Word. Pray God's promises aloud. Believe because He said so.

Prayer: *Thank You, Father, for continuity and constancy amidst a world of* confusion and chaos. I'm grateful to know You're always with me and never need an attitude adjustment before I talk to You. In Jesus' name, Amen.

Journal Page — Day Thirty-Two

The Lord Is Immutable

I the Lord do not change. Malachi 3:6 (NIV)

1. Describe your reaction to God's promise, "I the Lord do not change."

2. What changes have you experienced over the past year?

3. Are you quick or slow to adapt to change?

4. Is there something in your life you sense the Lord leading you to change? If so, pray for continued guidance to obey.

Additional Scriptures

God, who is enthroned from of old, who does not change — Psalm 55:19 (NIV)

Day Thirty-Three

THE LORD IS — GOD WHO GRANTS PEACE DESPITE FALSEHOOD

Keep falsehood and lies far from me. Proverbs 30:8a. (NIV)

Smack in the middle of a great evening, I received news of accusations against me that weren't true. The conversation left unrest, hurt, and frustrated sadness at how the real enemy distracted and destroyed families. For a while, I got lost, mulling over the angry words; then, a yearning for relief reminded me that others' lies and slander were outside my control circle. I sought peace from God.

King Solomon declared by God's inspiration that one should desire a good name more than great riches. Since a good reputation is so valuable, the Lord frowns on spreading malicious untruths about another person. Proverbs 6:16-19 lists seven things that God hates. Two include a false witness who pours out lies, which stirs up conflict in the community. Whether the community is your family, job, church, or friends, slander destroys fellowship and breaks trust. It's a poison that originated from God's enemy to disband unity.

If you're victimized by slanderous talk, remember God grants victory. Run to Him for peace and comfort. Every person will give an account of their words spoken. Use your tongue to build others up. Be diligent in guarding another's reputation by not receiving or sharing devious talk against them. Strive to follow the will of the God who grants peace from the nastiness of falsehood.

Prayer: *Father, may I live and speak according to Your will. Hearing bad things said when we know they're not true is frustrating. Thank You for knowing, understanding, and showing us how to live right despite untruths being spread about us. In Jesus' name, Amen.*

Journal Page — Day Thirty-Three

The Lord is — God Who Grants Peace Despite Falsehood

Keep falsehood and lies far from me. Proverbs 30:8a (NIV)

1. Has anyone lied about you? What was your initial reaction?

2. Have you told lies about someone? If so, what emotion welling from within caused you to speak those words?

3. What adverse effects did it cause the one(s) you spoke against?

4. Were you remorseful/sorry for voicing them after witnessing the destruction or other adverse consequences?

Additional Scriptures

Keep your tongue from evil and your lips from telling lies. Psalm 34:13 (NIV)

Day Thirty-Four

THE LORD IS – GOD WHO GRANTS UNDERSTANDING

Because they now understood the words that had been made known to them.
Nehemiah 8:12b (NIV)

Teal-colored bookshelves adorned an east wall, and a silver-gray area rug softened the wooden floor of my office area. I wanted to replace an old heavy desk that no longer fit a new, airy décor. One massive problem with switching would be finding a pre-assembled desk to avoid instructions and unfamiliar parts. My drill, screwdriver, and hammer skills require improvement. Sometimes assembly instructions read like a foreign language. A conversation between me, before spiritual maturity, and other parents popped into my mind. More than one of us lamented, "Kids should come with instructions."

Ezra prepared his heart to seek the law of the Lord. He purposed to obey and teach others to do the same. Jews and peers deemed him an expert on the law of Moses and well-versed in the office of priesthood and civil powers. I can imagine he fell asleep with excited anticipation. The following day, everyone gathered and listened to the Law of Moses. He'd studied the book. Nehemiah and the others would walk about the crowds to make sure each person understood, while he read. The Lord would enlighten. He'd commanded all who could understand to be present.

The desk search took patience and time, but I found a discontinued floor model. By attending Sunday school and Bible study, my faith matured. I realized that God's inspired Word is a detailed how-to manual. We hunger for the fellowship and strength gleaned from worship attendance, but deep learning occurs in the other two settings. It's okay to read a version other than King James to get an understanding. Parallel Bibles have two translations in one book. Choose a place and set aside time to spend with God. Start with prayer. Petition Him to open your eyes to view and comprehend every wondrous promise, word of encouragement, and correction needed to live your best life. The One who grants understanding will give liberally.

Prayer: *Father, I crave to understand Your Word and know You better. Please remove every distraction that attempts to deter me from spending quality and quantity time with You. In Jesus' name, Amen.*

Journal Page — Day Thirty-Four

The Lord is — God Who Grants Understanding

Because they now understood the words that had been made known to them. Nehemiah 8:12b (NIV)

1. Have you ever misread a recipe or directions on a medication label and mistaken the abbreviation for tablespoon (tbs.) for teaspoon (tsp.)? What were the results of the oversight?

2. Have you ever asked for directions and chosen to rely on memory, then forgot whether to turn left or right?

3. Why is it important to reflect on God's Word deeply?

4. Once we understand God's law, we should _____ it.

5. What could the books of the Bible and a handwritten letter from you to a loved one have in common?

6. Has someone ever misinterpreted or taken words you wrote or spoke out of context? What was your response then? Would it still be the same today?

Additional Scriptures

Your hands made me and formed me. Give me understanding to learn your commands. Psalm 119:73 (NIV)

Day Thirty-Five

THE LORD IS – THE GOD OF HUMILITY

You will be driven away from people and will live with the wild animals;
you will eat grass like the ox and be drenched with the dew of heaven. Seven times
will pass by for you until you acknowledge that the Most High is sovereign over
all kingdoms on earth and gives them to anyone he wishes. Daniel 4:25 (NIV)

A political candidate ran an aggressive advertising campaign, drenching the public with floods of promises superseded by the word "I." His social media ads boasted of past accolades but gave no credit to God, family, or constituents. I judged his attitude offensive. One day, a friend complimented my writing. Pride replied, "Thank you," before humility gave God the glory. That's how fast we forget that every perfect gift comes from above. "I can't do anything without the Lord."

Nebuchadnezzar, king of the Chaldeans, let a position puff his pride so high God sent a vision to deflate the balloon of haughtiness. The king dreamed that a great and fruitful tree was reduced to a stump in a grass field amongst beasts for seven years. Daniel, a faithful servant of God, told Nebuchadnezzar that the tree symbolized the king's life until he understood and acknowledged the true ruler. "You must know that the Most High rules in the kingdom of men and gives it to whomsoever He wills," Daniel warned. Nebuchadnezzar listened, but the dream no longer disturbed him as time passed.

Twelve months later, however, he strolled into the palace and glanced at all the finery, and the boasting monster struck again. I visualize him swirling about in his long robe, hands clasped behind his back, eyes darting about, shining with glee as they lighted on one opulent corner of the grand showcase with a smug grin. "I built all..." he started to say. Before he completed the sentence, a voice from heaven denounced him. Driven from the palace and men, the prideful king dwelt with beasts of the field, ate grass as oxen, and grew hair like eagle feathers and nails like bird claws. Why? He refused to recognize that our God Most High is the Lord of humility.

Picture an apple seed. With dirt, water, and sun from God, that seed will grow into a tree and produce apples. Without those essentials, it's just a seed. Humanity, like the seed, depends on blessings from the Lord. Humility starts when we know and accept our lowliness before His greatness. Spend routine time in self-examination to uncover and confess pride. Look for ways to serve others. Submit wholeheartedly to the God of humility.

Prayer: *Father, may I humbly beseech You for every need, knowing my very breath depends on You. In Jesus' name, Amen.*

Journal Page — Day Thirty-Five

The Lord is — The God of Humility

You will be driven away from people and will live with the wild animals; you will eat grass like the ox and be drenched with the dew of heaven. Seven times will pass by for you until you acknowledge that the Most High is sovereign over all kingdoms on earth and gives them to anyone he wishes. Daniel 4:25 (NIV)

1. What does it mean to be humble?

2. Write a word opposite of humble.

3. Who is the "you" the author is referring to in the above verse?

4. Why will the person suffer such consequences?

5. Define "sovereign" in your words.

6. Is pride an area of concern in any part of your life? If so, where? How will you get rid of it?

Ask God to search your heart and show you any hidden pride that may masquerade as humility. If you yell "ouch," don't fret. You're not alone. It's incredible what we learn when we yield ourselves to God. We're privileged children to bring every burden to our Father.

Additional Scriptures

But he gives us more grace. That is why Scripture says: God opposes the proud but shows favor to the humble. James 4:6 (NIV)

Day Thirty-Six

THE LORD IS – GOD OF THE CHILDLESS PARENT

Listen, my son, to your father's instruction, and do not forsake your mother's teaching. Proverbs 1:8 (NIV)

I have two friends, Kay and Deb, neither of whom have labored in childbirth, but God created each of these precious ladies with a mother's loving heart. Each has played an integral role, from auntie/second mom to nieces and nephews. Both have sharpened bright minds with the love of Jesus by teaching children's church and continue to influence teens and young adults. I marvel at their energy. One glimpse into their eyes, and you'll recognize that the love of God drives these mothers. Though childless by the womb, they're rich in motherhood.

Though single, Gary desired to be a daddy. Through his church's mentoring program, he met and fostered ten-year-old Ray. The adoption process trickled like thick syrup. Both were eager to be dad and son. Gary relied on teachings learned from his mom when he helped rear four siblings. The mentor-parenting approach challenged each young man to think and live as reflections of God based on Genesis 1:26-27.

Solomon, son of David, asked God for wisdom to know how to lead according to the Lord's will. He wrote Proverbs 1 and many others. He, like Moses, taught the Israelites to love and obey the Lord and teach their children the same reverence. The verse above commanded sons to listen, as in hear and follow their father's instructions. The children were admonished not to forsake the firsthand teachings viewed daily in their homes. The men were often out of the home working, tending business, or meeting at the city gate. Youth of the biblical days attended school at home and learned from relatives, friends, and neighbors.

Similar strategies are used to teach youth today in education and Sunday schools. Neither Kay nor Deb could have imagined the countless verbal, social media, plaque tributes, and testimonials each has acquired from grateful grown-ups. Nieces, nephews, and church family have grabbed and gathered them in bear hugs of humble appreciation, exclaiming, "You're like a second mama!" One said, "I'm thankful for all my mamas."

Gary endured a long quest to adopt Ray. The process compelled him to volunteer for CASA (Court Appointed Special Advocate) and devote time, energy, and insight to assisting foster children.

God's ways and thoughts are higher than we could ever attain. Maybe you or someone you know has a parent's heart and gobs of love to share. If so, seek the Lord's guidance on what that looks like. Ask a prayer warrior to join you. God knows your story. Trust Him. Know that you're made in His image, for a purpose, and with unique talents to glorify and honor God.

Prayer: *Lord, I pray that this devotional reaches the one You intended. May it heal and not hurt. May it edify and not tear down. May it inspire and draw the reader close to You. I trust You, now and forever, In Jesus' name, Amen.*

Journal Page — Day Thirty-Six

The Lord is — The God of The Childless Parent

Listen, my son, to your father's instruction, and do not forsake your mother's teaching. Proverbs 1:8 (NIV)

Reflection: I thought long and hard about the title of this one. I intend to build up God's people and glorify His name, so I won't offend. The title came from one of the ladies I wrote about. She didn't realize the gift she gave. I'm grateful to God for these examples.

1. What's your definition of a parent?

2. Name men and women who have positively influenced your life.

3. What parent or childless parent can you encourage?

4. Jewish worshippers sang Psalm 113 before one of their annual celebrations. Do you have a favorite worship song? If so, when do you sing it most often?

Prayer: *Father, please bless and use the precious vessel You ordained to sense a leading or purpose from this devotional. May Your glorious will be accomplished. In Jesus' name, Amen.*

Day Thirty-Seven

THE LORD IS — AUTHOR AND FINISHER OF MY STORY

Before I formed you in the womb, I knew you. Before you were born, I set you apart. I appointed you as a prophet to the nations. Jeremiah 1:5 (NIV)

Even before I knew Him, God authored me into existence. He planned for me to serve Him as an encourager to His people. Gifts were shaped to draw others to the Lord with free will. It's my prerogative to obey or refuse and suffer consequences. Genesis records that God patterned humanity in His image. We have a heart and soul fashioned to love as potently as our Father. Sometimes, I look back over my life and wonder, "Why didn't You protect a naïve person like me?" But how would I relate to those who need encouragement if the Lord had sheltered me from heartache, sorrow, and pain? Some decisions we may regret, some we laud, but each outcome and consequence has shaped us. One day in fourth grade, God authored a deep calling within me to write. The desire has evolved from a hunger to pen the great American romance to devotions that will touch hearts and glorify Him.

During the reign of twenty-one-year-old King Josiah, the Lord also ordained a young priest named Jeremiah to pronounce judgment on Judah. He delivered messages to the kingdom of Judah before, during, and after it fell to Babylon. Like Moses, the priest spouted several excuses to avoid the task: "I'm young and won't know what to speak."

The Lord, who'd chosen Jeremiah before He authored him in the womb, had a plan. "I set you apart before birth and purposed you as a prophet to the nations. Don't fear anyone. I will rescue you." (Jer. 1:5, 8) Prophets voiced words and followed instructions as God directed. This prophet witnessed much sorrow in Judah's downfall, Israel's destruction, and his personal life. The Lord God enabled the priest-prophet to edify Judah with a covenant of hope and restoration.

Merriam-Webster Dictionary defines an author as one who originates or creates something. Another online dictionary defined an author as someone who gave existence to anything and whose authorship determines responsibility for what was created.[1] That's the Lord and us. He authored us as sure as He gifted us faith. Isn't it cool that we're privileged to write our chapters, knowing that the Finisher will polish the ending? You can make the best of the life chapters in between. Live each day as unto the Lord. Love others even if it's not reciprocated. When you mess up, confess it.

Prayer: *Father, thank You for being the Author and Finisher of my story and faith. Thank You for working even when I couldn't see it to mold me more like You. In Jesus' name, Amen.*

---

1   Merriam-Webster.com   Dictionary,   Merriam-Webster, https://www.merriam-webster.com/dictionary/author. Accessed 10 Jan. 2025.

2. Bryan Collins. *Become A Writer Today*, Author | Become A Writer Today

Journal Page-Day Thirty-Seven

The Lord is — The Author and Finisher of My Story

"Before I formed you in the womb, I knew you. Before you were born, I set you apart. I appointed you as a prophet to the nations." Jeremiah 1:5 (NIV)

1. Who have you allowed to author the story of your life?

2. Have they written a few chapters or a significant portion of your book?

3. List two highlights in your story that still make you smile.

4. Define "refreshes" in your words.

5. What has God set you apart to fulfill?

6. List words to describe a reaction to God's "knowing you."

Additional Scriptures:

"For I know the plans I have for you," declares the Lord, *"plans to prosper you and not to harm you, plans to give you hope and a future."* Jeremiah 29:11 (NIV)

Day Thirty-Eight

THE LORD IS — I AM

God said to Moses, I Am who I Am. This is what you are to say to the Israelites: I Am has sent me to you. Exodus 3:14 (NIV)

Most of the time, the words flow in writing my devotions. They're lessons from the Father to me before I share them with others. Sometimes, a project won't come together no matter how hard I strive. The writing reads as if stilted and forced. That's when doubt trickles in like a leaky faucet. I can relate to Moses' shyness when God chose him to speak and lead. I know He has gifted me the ability to write, yet thoughts of self-doubt come to mind, like, "Who am I to think I can pen words to tell people who God is?"

Egypt and Pharoah were a part of Moses' unpleasant past, and he desired to keep it that way. God called him from a fiery bush to rescue a nation of people. Moses understood and sympathized with the plight of the Israelites oppressed by brutal slavery. Hadn't he defended a fellow Israelite from an Egyptian? That Egyptian had died, and Moses fled to Midian, fearing retribution. God knew his past. How could He send him back to Pharaoh, let alone demand to the tyrant, "Let my people go!" Who would he say sent him?

God replied, "I Am that I Am. Tell them I Am sent you." He also assured Moses that the assigned task would succeed with a promise, "When you have brought the people from Israel, you will worship on this mountain." The Lord from before time began, and who would always be, promised. The One who spoke the world into existence created every living thing and caused a fiery bush to neither smoke nor be consumed, declared, "I Am He who has called and equipped you for this mission. Never will I leave nor forsake you. I have plans for you to do good work and finish it to completion." The God, I Am, supplied all required to accomplish His will.

My best writing times occur after reading and studying the Word because I'm plugged into my power source, God. Thoughts of self-doubt and whispers of insecurity from the enemy shrink away under the shield of faith and the sword of the Spirit.

Biblical history illustrates that most of the men and women God used were not prepared for the trials or the labor they were assigned. Let's

147

reflect on what it took for Moses and others to press on despite personal shortcomings. They had to maintain a close fellowship with the Lord and talk to and listen to Him to gain spiritual discernment. They had to read and meditate on scripture as if their lives depended on it. They did.

We should do the same as Moses and others, plus memorize verses that resonate. Trust what the Lord says. Do your best in every endeavor as if working for the Lord because you do. Finally, in everything, give thanks, knowing that the God I Am is in control.

Prayer: *I Am, thank You. Though our lips might utter words, none could express how grateful we are to belong to the One who can do all. Hallelujah, Amen.*

Journal Page — Day Thirty-Eight

The Lord is — I AM

God said to Moses, I Am who I Am. This is what you are to say to the Israelites: I Am has sent me to you. Exodus 3:14 (NIV)

1. Read aloud the first two words of the verse above several times. What does it mean to you that God spoke to Moses?

2. What has the great I Am called you to do that you don't feel equipped for?

3. Is there a reason this devotion might resonate, especially for you right now?

4. Picture the most significant obstacle you or someone you care about are facing. Close your eyes and repeat, "I Am is greater." Think about how huge the name of God is. He is so big and magnificent, so beyond our comprehension, that He *is*. God is greater than any obstacle against you.

Additional Scriptures

You are my portion, Lord. I have promised to obey your words. Psalm 119:57 (NIV)

Day Thirty-Nine

THE LORD IS — OUR DWELLING PLACE

Lord, You have been our dwelling place throughout all generations. Psalm 90:1 (NIV)

Fentanyl drug abuse, hunger, and a growing lack of trust in government plague our nation. An influx of news on these dire situations, mingled with my trials, could cause despair if not for God, my dwelling place.

Moses described God as his dwelling place in Psalm 90, the oldest Psalm in the book. Multiple online dictionaries define "dwelling" as a place where one lives or a permanent residence, and the Bible interchanges it with the word "refuge." Psalm 90:1 proclaims the Lord God as man's dwelling place since the beginning of creation.

Moses may have written this song after a forty-year wilderness journey with rebellious people. God served as a dwelling place of wisdom and protection and provided sustenance for Moses during the entire trek.

The meek-mannered leader experienced three tragedies in a short time. In the fortieth year of travel, his sister, Miriam, and brother, Aaron, died, and he lost permission to enter the Promised Land. Perhaps through the lens of sorrow, Moses comprehended the depth of comfort in God's constant presence and the brevity of life. He pleaded that the Israelites might understand also. "Teach us to number our days, that we may gain a heart of wisdom." Psalm 90:12

When I'm home, the television stays off until five o'clock for the news. My favorite segments include the weather and the final minute, which ends the cast on a positive note. Troubling stories still provoke sad reactions. Instead of stomach-twisting angst, I dwell in the eternal God for peace and assurance.

When giants of trouble plague and threaten to overwhelm you, shift your view to an eternal focus. The Lord is still a dwelling place of peace and all you need. Make the best of each day. Life is short and precious. Stay thankful and prayerful in every situation.

Prayer: *From the rising of the sun to the going down of the same, Lord, we thank You that You never change. You are eternal, powerful, and our dwelling place. In Jesus' name, Amen.*

Journal Page — Day Thirty-Nine

The Lord Is — Our Dwelling Place

Lord, you have been our dwelling place throughout all generations. Psalm 90:1 (NIV)

1. Define "eternal" in your words.

2. What comes to mind when you picture refuge?

3. How is God your dwelling place?

4. In what area of your life do you need God to drive out the enemies, i.e., mind distractions?

5. What does "God's everlasting arms" mean to you?

Additional Scriptures

He will cover you with his feathers, and you will find refuge under his wings. His faithfulness will be your shield and rampart. Psalm 91:4 (NIV)

Day Forty

THE LORD IS — OUR FATHER

Yet you, Lord, are our Father. Isaiah 64:8 (NIV)

A wealth of cards line shelves for Mother's Day, but the choices are slimmer in June for Father's Day. One store clerk remarked, "We don't sell many of them because many have daddy issues." I'd never considered that before. Outside the store, I paused to give thanks for the gift of my earthly daddy and for my Father God, who is a Father to all.

Through David's writings in the book of Psalms, God has taught me much about the close relationship between the two. As the young shepherd boy advanced into adulthood, he experienced new challenges of jealousy from King Saul.

Emotions of fear and separation anxiety shrouded David on the run for his life. Journaling all that roiled in his mind and heart helped the future king sort out his feelings. Those feelings and requests transformed into a diary of songs to the sovereign Father. David longed for a strong embrace from his earthly dad, Jesse. The lad strained to remember his voice or words of advice. Did you know that the Lord above is the Father of comfort who cares for the orphaned and widowed? For sure, He understood David's sorrow and angst. Visualize the king, heartbroken and contrite for the sins of adultery and murder, offering sincere sacrifices of repentance to his divine Father who would chasten him.

Take the route along Psalm 139 to discover that our heavenly Father sees the good and not-so-good deeds done in the dark yet still loves us. He provided for David's every need, counseled and encouraged him without condition, and, sweetest of all, as night comes when no man can work, our Father will ensure we arrive at our home eternal.

My Dad is deceased now, so Father's Day brings a sad yearning mingled with joy at knowing where he is. Whether our fellowship with our earthly fathers has dissolved due to death or difficulties, we still have a Father who cares for us. The conversation with the store clerk about greeting cards gave more profound meaning to God's promise to be a Father to the orphaned and widowed.

Resolve to give others more grace. We don't know the hardships they've endured as children. There's a story and a reason behind every action. A person with unhealed hurts, habits, or hangups may carry that into a relationship, whether marriage or parenting. God loves you. He is your Father who will never leave nor reject you, longs to spend time with you and knows every hair on your head. Talk to Him. Listen. He will answer you. Your Heavenly Father can supply healing through His Word and guidance via a licensed counselor or peer group.

Prayer: *Father, so many have suffered unimaginable pain at the hands of another hurt human being. Please heal their wounds and show them that You are real. Use us as Your vessels of love and mercy. In Jesus' name, Amen.*

Journal Page — Day Forty

The Lord Is My Father

Yet you, Lord, are our Father. Isaiah 64:8 (NIV)

1. Is your fellowship with God as close as you would like? Explain

2. How often do you talk aloud to God? Is there a significance to talking aloud?

3. What does quiet time with the Father mean to you?

4. Do you want to know God better or know about God? What's the difference?

5. In Psalm 139:23, David asked God to search him and know his heart and anxious thoughts. Are you willing to surrender your heart and every anxious thought to a Father who loves you without conditions? How will you start?

Additional Scriptures

As a father has compassion on his children, so the Lord has compassion on those who fear him. Psalm 103:13 (NIV)

MEET THE AUTHOR

Sharon Simms is a grateful believer in Jesus Christ who adores family, friends, and people in general. The Lord altered her childhood dream of writing a best-selling novel and amassing riches to pen passionate devotions that showcase His love and promises. Her greatest passions are to please God and spread the Gospel. Sharon posts daily devotional vlogs on *www.sharondsimms.com*, YouTube, and Instagram. She resides in the piney woods of East Texas and thrives on being an agent of joy and encouragement for Jesus.

Thank You

Thank you for reading this book from Mt. Zion Ridge Press.

If you enjoyed the experience, learned something, gained a new perspective, or made new friends through story, could you do us a favor and write a review on Goodreads or wherever you bought the book?

Thanks! We and our authors appreciate it.

We invite you to visit our website, MtZionRidgePress.com, and explore other titles in fiction and non-fiction. We always have something coming up that's new and off the beaten path.

And please check out our podcast, **Books on the Ridge,** where we chat with our authors and give them a chance to share what was in their hearts while they wrote their book, as well as fun anecdotes and glimpses into their lives and experiences and the writing process. And we always discuss a very important topic: *Tea!*

You can listen to the podcast on our website or find it at most of the usual places where podcasts are available online. Please subscribe so you don't miss a single episode!

Thanks for reading. We hope you come back soon!